AAT

AQ2016

Personal Tax
(Finance Act 2020)

EXAM KIT

This Exam Kit supports study for the following AAT qualifications:
AAT Professional Diploma in Accounting – Level 4
AAT Level 4 Diploma in Business Skills
AAT Professional Diploma in Accounting at SCQF Level 8

KAPLAN

PUBLISHING

British Library Cataloguing-in-Publication Data

A catalogue record for this book is available from the British Library.

Published by:

Kaplan Publishing UK

Unit 2 The Business Centre

Molly Millar's Lane

Wokingham

Berkshire

RG41 2QZ

ISBN: 978-1-78740-809-8

© Kaplan Financial Limited, 2020

Printed and bound in Great Britain.

CONTENTS

Features in this exam kit

In addition to providing a wide ranging bank of real assessment style questions, we have also included in this kit:

- unit specific information and advice on assessment technique

- our recommended approach to make your revision for this particular unit as effective as possible.

You will find a wealth of other resources to help you with your studies on the Kaplan and AAT websites:

www.mykaplan.co.uk

www.aat.org.uk/

Quality and accuracy are of the utmost importance to us so if you spot an error in any of our products, please send an email to mykaplanreporting@kaplan.com with full details, or follow the link to the feedback form in MyKaplan.

Our Quality Coordinator will work with our technical team to verify the error and take action to ensure it is corrected in future editions.

INDEX TO QUESTIONS AND ANSWERS

KAPLAN PUBLISHING

INHERITANCE TAX

ANSWER ENHANCEMENTS

We have added the following enhancements to the answers in this exam kit:

Key answer tips

Some answers include key answer tips to help your understanding of each question.

Tutorial note

Some answers include tutorial notes to explain some of the technical points in more detail.

ASSESSMENT TECHNIQUE

- **Do not skip any of the material** in the syllabus.

- **Read each question** *very* carefully.

- **Double-check your answer** before committing yourself to it.

- Answer **every** question – if you do not know an answer to a multiple choice question or true/false question, you don't lose anything by guessing. Think carefully before you **guess**.

- If you are answering a multiple-choice question, **eliminate first those answers that you know are wrong**. Then choose the most appropriate answer from those that are left.

- **Don't panic** if you realise you've answered a question incorrectly. Getting one question wrong will not mean the difference between passing and failing

Computer-based assessments – tips

- Do not attempt a CBA until you have **completed all study material** relating to it.

- On the AAT website there is a CBA demonstration. It is **ESSENTIAL** that you attempt this before your real CBA. You will become familiar with how to move around the CBA screens and the way that questions are formatted, increasing your confidence and speed in the actual assessment.

- Be sure you understand how to use the **software** before you start the assessment. If in doubt, ask the assessment centre staff to explain it to you.

- Questions are **displayed on the screen** and answers are entered using keyboard and mouse. At the end of the assessment, you are given a certificate showing the result you have achieved unless some manual marking is required for the assessment.

- In addition to the traditional multiple-choice question type, CBAs will also contain **other types of questions,** such as number entry questions, drag and drop, true/false, pick lists or drop down menus or hybrids of these.

- In some CBAs you may have to type in complete computations or written answers.

- You need to be sure you **know how to answer questions** of this type before you sit the real assessment, through practice.

UNIT SPECIFIC INFORMATION

THE ASSESSMENT

FORMAT OF THE ASSESSMENT

Students will be assessed by computer-based assessment.

In any one assessment, students may not be assessed on all content, or on the full depth or breadth of a piece of content. The content assessed may change over time to ensure validity of assessment, but all assessment criteria will be tested over time.

The learning outcomes for this unit are as follows:

	Learning outcome	Weighting
1	Analyse the theories, principles and rules that underpin taxation systems	10%
2	Calculate a UK taxpayer's total income	28%
3	Calculate income tax and National Insurance (NI) contributions payable by a UK taxpayer	23%
4	Account for capital gains tax	27%
5	Discuss the basics of inheritance tax	12%
	Total	100%

Time allowed

2 hours 30 minutes

AAT SAMPLE ASSESSMENT

Task	Learning outcome	Topic
1	1.2, 1.3	Professional conduct in relation to taxation
2	2.1	Employment income benefits – provision of cars
3	2.1	Employment income benefits – other benefits
4	2.2	Investment income
5	2.3	Income from property
6	3.1, 3.2, 3.3	Calculation of income tax liability
7	3.4	National insurance contributions
8	3.5	Minimising tax
9	4.1, 4.2	Knowledge of capital gains tax

Kaplan Publishing are constantly finding new ways to make a difference to your studies and our exciting online resources really do offer something different to students looking for exam success.

This book comes with free MyKaplan online resources so that you can study anytime, anywhere. **This free online resource is not sold separately and is included in the price of the book.**

Having purchased this book, you have access to the following online study materials:

CONTENT	AAT	
	Text	Kit
Electronic version of the book	✓	✓
Progress tests with instant answers	✓	
Mock assessments online	✓	✓
Material updates	✓	✓

How to access your online resources

Kaplan Financial students will already have a MyKaplan account and these extra resources will be available to you online. You do not need to register again, as this process was completed when you enrolled. If you are having problems accessing online materials, please ask your course administrator.

If you are not studying with Kaplan and did not purchase your book via a Kaplan website, to unlock your extra online resources please go to www.mykaplan.co.uk/addabook (even if you have set up an account and registered books previously). You will then need to enter the ISBN number (on the title page and back cover) and the unique pass key number contained in the scratch panel below to gain access. You will also be required to enter additional information during this process to set up or confirm your account details.

If you purchased through the Kaplan Publishing website you will automatically receive an e-mail invitation to MyKaplan. Please register your details using this email to gain access to your content. If you do not receive the e-mail or book content, please contact Kaplan Publishing.

Your Code and Information

This code can only be used once for the registration of one book online. This registration and your online content will expire when the final sittings for the examinations covered by this book have taken place. Please allow one hour from the time you submit your book details for us to process your request.

Please scratch the film to access your unique code.

RlZX-UrvC-eDZs-vX5B

Please be aware that this code is case-sensitive and you will need to include the dashes within the passcode, but not when entering the ISBN.

KAPLAN

PUBLISHING

10	4.3	Chargeable gain on a disposal of shares
11	4.4	Calculation of capital gains tax
12	5.1	Knowledge of inheritance tax
13	5.2	Calculation of inheritance tax

GUIDANCE FROM CHIEF ASSESSOR

The chief assessor has stated prior to AQ2016 that 'Learners cannot avoid any of the key topics and to ensure success, must be prepared to answer written and computational style questions in any of the tasks.' This advice is still applicable under AQ2016.

PASS MARK

The pass mark for all AAT CBAs is 70%.

 Always keep your eye on the clock and make sure you attempt all questions!

DETAILED SYLLABUS

The detailed syllabus and study guide written by the AAT can be found at:

www.aat.org.uk/

ASSESSMENT GUIDANCE

- Some questions ask that answers be calculated to the nearest £. Some answers may require learners to calculate to the nearest £ and pence. If the question does not give any instructions then either method is acceptable and the computer will accept both.

- Some questions have scroll bars at the side. It is important that learners scroll down and do not miss out parts of questions.

- Where free text written answers are required, learners are supplied with a box to type their answers. This scrolls down as far as is necessary to accommodate the learner's answer.

- It is very important to read questions carefully. Common errors which have occurred in the assessments are:

  (i)   Not spotting when salaries are given monthly and not annually

  (ii)   Misreading dates

  (iii) Being unable to work out the number of months in a period when time apportionment is required (e.g. if a salary changes on 1 November then there are 7 months of the old salary and 5 of the new).

- Learners often muddle up the contributions by employees when calculating car and fuel benefits.

KAPLAN'S RECOMMENDED REVISION APPROACH

QUESTION PRACTICE IS THE KEY TO SUCCESS

Success in professional examinations relies upon you acquiring a firm grasp of the required knowledge at the tuition phase. In order to be able to do the questions, knowledge is essential.

However, the difference between success and failure often hinges on your assessment technique on the day and making the most of the revision phase of your studies.

The **Kaplan study text** is the starting point, designed to provide the underpinning knowledge to tackle all questions. However, in the revision phase, poring over text books is not the answer.

Kaplan pocket notes are designed to help you quickly revise a topic area; however you then need to practise questions. There is a need to progress to assessment style questions as soon as possible, and to tie your assessment technique and technical knowledge together.

The importance of question practice cannot be over-emphasised.

The recommended approach below is designed by expert tutors in the field, in conjunction with their knowledge of the chief assessor and the sample assessment.

You need to practise as many questions as possible in the time you have left.

OUR AIM

Our aim is to get you to the stage where you can attempt assessment questions confidently, to time, in a closed book environment, with no supplementary help (i.e. to simulate the real assessment experience).

Practising your assessment technique is also vitally important for you to assess your progress and identify areas of weakness that may need more attention in the final run up to the real assessment.

In order to achieve this we recognise that initially you may feel the need to practise some questions with open book help.

Good assessment technique is vital.

THE KAPLAN PLTX REVISION PLAN

Stage 1: Assess areas of strength and weakness

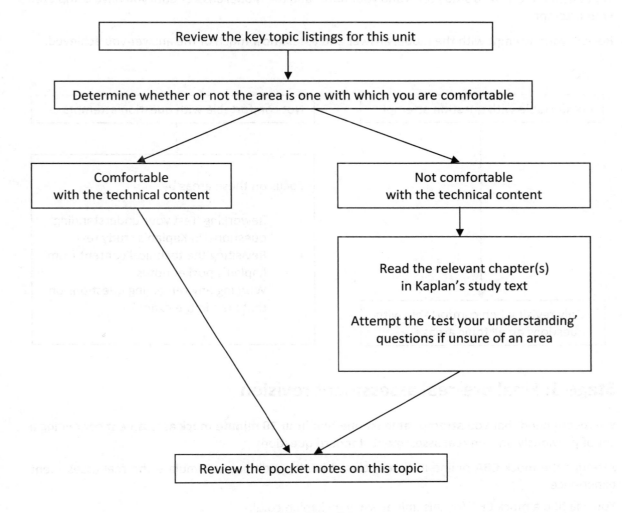

Stage 2: Practice questions

Follow the order of revision of topics as presented in this kit and attempt the questions in the order suggested.

Try to avoid referring to study texts and your notes and the model answer until you have completed your attempt.

Review your attempt with the model answer and assess how much of the answer you achieved.

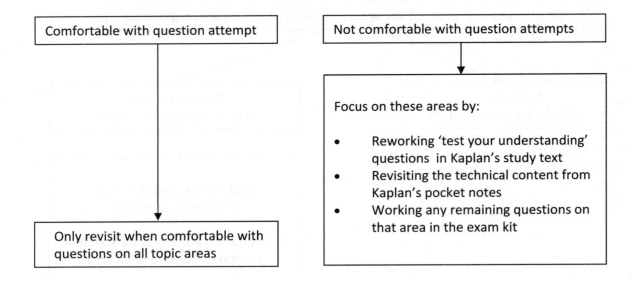

Comfortable with question attempt	Not comfortable with question attempts

Focus on these areas by:

- Reworking 'test your understanding' questions in Kaplan's study text
- Revisiting the technical content from Kaplan's pocket notes
- Working any remaining questions on that area in the exam kit

Only revisit when comfortable with questions on all topic areas

Stage 3: Final pre-real assessment revision

We recommend that you **attempt at least one two hour 30 minute mock assessment** containing a set of previously unseen real assessment standard questions.

Attempt the mock CBA online in timed, closed book conditions to simulate the real assessment experience.

You will find a mock CBA for this unit at www.mykaplan.co.uk

TAX RATES AND ALLOWANCES

Throughout this exam kit:

1   You should assume that the tax rates and allowances for the tax year 2020/21 will continue to apply for the foreseeable future unless you are instructed otherwise.

2   Calculations should be made to the nearest £ unless the question states otherwise.

3   All apportionments should be made to the nearest month.

Tax rates and allowances similar to those below will be reproduced in the assessment for personal tax.

In addition, other specific information necessary for candidates to answer individual questions will be given as part of the question.

Tax rates and bands

Rates	Bands	Normal rates %	Dividend rates %
Basic rate	£1 - £37,500	20	7.5
Higher rate	£37,501 - £150,000	40	32.5
Additional rate	£150,001 and over	45	38.1

Allowances

		£
Personal allowance		12,500
Savings allowance	Basic rate taxpayer	1,000
	Higher rate taxpayer	500
Dividend allowance		2,000
Income limit for personal allowances[1]		100,000

[[1] Personal allowances are reduced by £1 for every £2 over the income limit]

Property allowance

Annual limit	£1,000

Individual savings accounts

Annual limit	£20,000

Car benefit percentage

CO2 Emissions for petrol engines g/km	Electric range Miles	Cars first registered from 6 April 2020 %
Nil		0
1 to 50	130 or more	0
1 to 50	70 - 129	3
1 to 50	40 - 69	6
1 to 50	30 – 39	10
1 to 50	Less than 30	12
51 to 54		13
55 or more		14 + 1% for every 5g/km over 55g/km
Registration pre 6 April 2020*		Additional 2%
Diesel engines**		Additional 4%

* The additional 2% does not apply to pure electric vehicles

** The additional 4% will not apply to diesel cars which are registered after 1 September 2017 and meet the RDE2 standards.

Car fuel benefit

Base figure	£24,500

Approved mileage allowance payments (employees and residential landlords)

First 10,000 miles	45p per mile
Over 10,000 miles	25p per mile
Additional passengers	5p per mile per passenger
Motorcycles	24p per mile
Bicycles	20p per mile

Van scale charge

Basic charge	£3,490
Private fuel charge	£666
Benefit charge for zero-emission vans	80%

Other benefits in kind

Expensive accommodation limit	£75,000
Health screening	One per year
Incidental overnight expenses: within the UK	£5 per night
Incidental overnight expenses: overseas	£10 per night
Job-related accommodation	£Nil
Living expenses where job-related exemption applies	Restricted to 10% of employees net earnings
Loan of assets annual charge	20%
Low-rate or interest free loans	Up to £10,000
Mobile telephones	One per employee
Non-cash gifts from someone other than the employer	£250 per tax year
Non-cash long service award	£50 per year of service
Pay whilst attending a full time course	£15,480 per academic year
Provision of eye tests and spectacles for VDU use	£Nil
Provision of parking spaces	£Nil
Provision of workplace childcare	£Nil
Provision of workplace sports facilities	£Nil
Removal and relocation expenses	£8,000
Staff party or event	£150 per head
Staff suggestion scheme	Up to £5,000
Subsidised meals	£Nil
Working from home	£6 per week / £26 per month

HMRC official rate	2.25%

National insurance contributions

		%
Class 1 employee	Below £9,500	0
	Above £9,500 and below £50,000	12
	£50,000 and above	2
Class 1 employer	Below £8,788	0
	£8,788 and above	13.8
Class 1A		13.8
Employment allowance		£4,000

Capital gains tax

Annual exempt amount	£12,300

Tax rates

Basic rate	10%
Higher rate	20%

Inheritance tax – tax rates

Nil rate band	£325,000
Additional residence nil rate band[3]	£175,000

		%
Excess taxable at:	Death rate	40
	Lifetime rate	20

[3 Applies when a home is passed on death to direct descendants of the deceased after 6 April 2017. Any unused band is transferrable to a spouse or civil partner.]

Inheritance tax – tapering relief

	% reduction
3 years or less	0
Over 3 years but less than 4 years	20
Over 4 years but less than 5 years	40
Over 5 years but less than 6 years	60
Over 6 years but less than 7 years	80

Inheritance tax – exemptions

		£
Small gifts		250 per transferee per tax year
Marriage or civil partnership:	From parent	5,000
	From grandparent	2,500
	From one party to the other	2,500
	From others	1,000
Annual exemption		3,000

Deemed domicile	Criteria
Condition A	Was born in the UK
	Domicile of origin was in the UK
	Was resident in the UK for 2017 to 2018 or later years
Condition B	Has been UK resident for at least 15 of the 20 years immediately before the relevant tax year

Section 1

PRACTICE QUESTIONS

TAXATION AND THE TAX ADVISER

Key answer tips

Professional conduct in relation to taxation is covered in task 1 of the sample assessment. All or part of this question may require a free text written response. The task may have one or more parts. The questions in this section of the kit give practice on the individual question parts that you may see in this task.

It is essential that you practice all free text written questions provided as this is an area where students often do not perform well in the exam.

The AAT document 'Professional conduct in relation to taxation' is available for you to refer to in the assessment. You must be very familiar with the layout of this document and the various areas covered so that you are able to find the information you need. You should then practise all of the questions and, where appropriate, write out complete answers. This will ensure that you are comfortable applying the guidance to the facts in the question.

1   PROFESSIONAL CONDUCT IN RELATION TO TAXATION (1)

Are the following statements true or false in connection with a tax adviser's professional conduct?

Tick the appropriate box for each statement.

	True	False
The duty of confidentiality applies to existing clients but not to ex-clients		
There is no obligation to comply with an informal request for information from HM Revenue and Customs		
A client's tax adviser has the primary responsibility for ensuring that the tax return is correct before it is submitted		
Tax evasion is acceptable where the tax being charged is unreasonable		

2   PROFESSIONAL CONDUCT IN RELATION TO TAXATION (2)

Are the following statements true or false in connection with a tax adviser's professional conduct?

Tick the appropriate box for each statement.

	True	False
It is acceptable for a tax return to include an estimated figure as opposed to one that is precise		
It is up to the client to decide whether or not a particular tax-planning strategy is appropriate		
A notification to HM Revenue and Customs that a tax adviser has ceased to act for a client must include a reason for the adviser's action		
Confidential information must never be disclosed without the client's specific permission		

3   PROFESSIONAL CONDUCT IN RELATION TO TAXATION (3)

Are the following statements true or false in connection with a tax adviser's professional conduct?

Tick the appropriate box for each statement.

	True	False
A tax adviser is obliged to provide any information which has been requested by HM Revenue and Customs		
It is acceptable for a tax adviser to provide assistance to a person who has been accused of tax evasion		
It is essential that a client reviews their tax return before it is submitted, even if the client's affairs are very simple		
It is up to the client to decide whether or not particular information should be disclosed to HM Revenue and Customs		

4   MICROMATTERS LTD

You are employed by a firm of accountants. Your firm has received a statutory (legal) request for information from HM Revenue and Customs in relation to Micromatters Ltd, one of the firm's clients.

Using the AAT guidelines 'Professional conduct in relation to taxation', explain your responsibilities in relation to this matter.

5   CORA

You work for a firm of accountants. You have seen a report in the local newspaper concerning Cora, a client of your firm. The report concerned the recent sale of a painting for £410,000. The report claimed that the painting was owned by Cora for many years until she sold it to the current vendor on 1 May 2018. There is no mention in Cora's 2018/19 tax return of a painting being sold.

Using the AAT guidelines 'Professional conduct in relation to taxation', explain your responsibilities in relation to this matter.

6   TOM

(a)   Tom has been a client of your firm for a number of years. You have recently discovered that Tom has omitted to include the income received from his Irish rental property in his income tax return. When you contact Tom to discuss this he has refused to make any amendments stating that any errors in the tax return are not his problem.

Using the AAT guidelines 'Professional conduct in relation to taxation', explain the respective responsibilities of your firm and Tom in relation to his tax return.

(b)   **Your manager has suggested that Tom's attitude suggests the possibility of tax evasion here. Explain the meaning of the terms 'tax evasion' and 'tax planning' and whether the firm can be involved with returns involving evidence of each.**

7   SOFIA

Sofia is a manager in the accountancy firm you work at. She has developed a tax planning scheme that she believes can reduce the tax liabilities of a number of clients in your firm. She has been discussing it with other employees in the office and believes it will be highly profitable as it can be used for many taxpayers without adjustments. The scheme relies on an interpretation of tax legislation that has not yet been provided in Court, however HMRC have already indicated that they do not prescribe to this interpretation.

Using the AAT guidelines 'Professional Conduct in relation to taxation', explain the impact of the Standards for Tax Planning, in relation to this scheme.

8   ETHICAL RULES

(a)   **Which ONE of the following statements is not correct?**

A   Accountants should not be involved with tax returns that omit crucial information

B   Accountants should not be associated with a return that contains misleading information

C   Accountants who are involved with returns that deliberately contain false information can be subject to a penalty

D   Accountants should never prepare tax returns for clients

(b) **When can an accountant divulge confidential information?**

A If the information is over 6 years old

B If a member of the public asks for it

C If the accountant has written authority from the client to disclose

D If the client's spouse requests the information

9 CLIENT ADVICE

(a) **Which ONE of the following statements is not correct?**

A Accountants are responsible for preparing an accurate tax return based on the information provided by the client

B Accountants can break the rules of confidentiality when the public interest is threatened

C Tax evasion is a legal means of reducing your tax liability

D The AAT expects its members to maintain an objective outlook

(b) **When an accountant is advising a client, to whom does he owe the greatest duty of care?**

A The accountant's employer

B The AAT

C The client

D The government

10 AAT STUDENT

(a) **Which of the following statements is not correct?**

A As a student of the AAT you are bound by the duty of confidentiality

B The rules of confidentiality do not need to be followed when a wife asks for information about her husband's tax matters

C The rules of confidentiality need to be followed even after the client relationship has ended

D Confidentiality means not disclosing information you acquire due to your job

(b) **When an accountant is working for a client, when can the rules of confidentiality be breached?**

A If you do not agree with what the client is saying

B If the client refuses to correct an error in their tax return

C If you resign

D If the client is suspected of money laundering

11 NASHEEN

Nasheen is a student member of the AAT. She asks whether the following statements are true or false.

Tick the appropriate box for each statement.

	True	False
If a husband is ill, it is acceptable to discuss his tax affairs with his wife even if no letter of authorisation exists		
Accountants must maintain confidentiality irrespective of the situation		

12 RESIDENCE AND DOMICILE

Are the following statements true or false?

Tick the appropriate box for each statement.

	True	False
An individual is originally domiciled in the country in which he is born		
Individuals who are not resident in the UK may still be subject to UK income tax		
An individual is automatically resident in the UK if they own a second home in the UK		
An individual whose domicile of origin is France and who has lived in the UK since 2003/04, will be treated as deemed domiciled in the UK		

13 TAX SYSTEMS

Are the following statements true or false?

Tick the appropriate box for each statement.

	True	False
National insurance is a regressive tax		
Inheritance tax is an indirect tax		
Proportional taxes take an increasing proportion of income as income rises		

14   GERAN

Complete the following sentences using the words/numbers on the right.

Tick the appropriate column for each of the sentences.

UK income only	Overseas income only	UK and overseas income

1   Geran is resident in the UK.
    He will be subject to UK income tax on his ....

5	8	11

2   In 2020/21, Hogan has been in the UK for 175 days.
    If Hogan spends a further .... days in the UK he will automatically be UK resident.

16	46	91

3   Irene works full-time in France.
    Irene will be automatically non-UK resident if she is in the UK for less than .... days in the tax year.

15   RESIDENCY STATUS

Explain whether or not the following individuals are resident in the UK in the tax year 2020/21.

1   Kanu was born in Argentina. He lived in Argentina until the tax year 2020/21 when he came to the UK to visit for 40 days.

2   Lara was born in France. She lived in her home town in France until the tax year 2020/21. In 2020/21 she spent 40 weekends in the UK. Lara is employed full-time in France.

3   Mavis has always lived in the UK.

    In 2020/21 she went on a trip to travel the world. She travelled continuously for almost a year, returning to her house (her only home) in the UK on 5 May 2021. During 2020/21 she only spent 40 days in the UK, staying in her home.

INCOME TAX

TAXABLE BENEFITS – PROVISION OF CARS

Key answer tips

Task 2 in the sample assessment tests knowledge of car and fuel benefits. Calculating the benefit in respect of the provision of a car is tricky and there are many rules to learn. You will need to take great care when calculating these benefits in order to get them right.

16   SNAPE

Snape's employer gave him the choice of four company cars for 2020/21 with differing levels of CO_2 emissions. All the cars have petrol engines and the car chosen will be registered on 6 April 2020 and provided to Snape from that date.

(a)   **Calculate the appropriate car benefit percentage that will be applied for each car?**

(i)	54 g/km
(ii)	111 g/km
(iii)	134 g/km
(iv)	224 g/km

(b)   Snape chose the car with 134 g/km of emissions, but when it arrived it was a diesel engine car not petrol. The car does not meet the RDE2 standards.

The car cost the employer £21,000 but this was with a discount of £995 from the original list price of £21,995.

The company pays for all running costs including the fuel although Snape contributes £50 per month towards private fuel.

(i) What is the appropriate car benefit percentage for this car?	%
(ii) What is the cost of the car to use in the taxable benefit calculation?	£
(iii) What is the standard amount on which fuel benefit is calculated?	£
(iv) What is Snape's fuel benefit?	£

17   SAM

(a)   **Which percentage would be applied to calculate the taxable benefit for cars with the following CO_2 emissions? None of the cars meet the RDE2 standards and all will be registered on 6 April 2020.**

(i)   Petrol hybrid (electric range 39 miles) 26g/km

(ii)   Diesel 79 g/km

(iii)   Diesel 139 g/km

(iv)   Petrol 202 g/km

(b)   Sam was provided with a second hand company car in March 2020.

When he received the car it had a market value of £23,000 but the car's list price when registered in October 2019 was £27,000. The car has CO_2 emissions of 134 g/km and has a diesel engine that does not meet the RDE2 standards.

In 2020/21 the company spent £750 on servicing and repairing the car, £620 on insurance and road tax and £2,000 on fuel for business trips.

Sam is not reimbursed for any of his private diesel costs.

(i)	What is the appropriate car benefit percentage for this car?	%
(ii)	What is the cost of the car to use in the taxable benefit calculation?	£
(iii)	What is the amount of car running costs taxed on Sam in 2020/21?	£

18   FRODO

Frodo was provided with a petrol engine company car on 5 August 2020, the day after it was registered.

The car cost the company £24,000 but its list price was £26,000. The car has CO_2 emissions of 117 g/km. The company pays all running costs including fuel.

Frodo pays £100 per month to his employer which is £70 in respect of his private use of the car and £30 as a contribution towards his private fuel costs.

(a)   What is the price used in calculating the car benefit?

A   £24,000

B   £26,000

(b)   What is the appropriate % used to calculate the car benefit

%

(c)   What is Frodo's taxable car benefit for 2020/21?

£

(d)   What is Frodo's taxable fuel benefit for 2020/21?

£

19   BARRY

(a)   Barry was provided with a newly registered company car in January 2020.

The company paid the list price of £27,000 for the car but Barry contributed £6,000 to the company towards the purchase price. The car has a diesel engine, CO_2 emissions of 126 g/km and does not meet the RDE2 standards.

The company pays all the running costs of £1,650 per annum but does not pay any private fuel costs to Barry. Barry pays £50 per month to his employer for the private use of the car.

(i)	What is the appropriate car benefit percentage for this car?	%
(ii)	What is the cost of the car to use in the taxable benefit calculation?	£
(iii)	What is Barry's taxable car benefit for 2020/21?	£

(b)   Crouch has a company car with a list price of £20,000 which is taxed using an appropriate car benefit percentage of 24%. The car was first provided on 1 September 2020.

Crouch has all his private fuel paid for by the company although he reimburses the company 50% of the cost each month. The total private fuel cost (before deducting Crouch's contribution) is £2,920 for 2020/21.

What is Crouch's fuel benefit for 2020/21?

A   £5,880

B   £3,430

C   £1,970

D   £1,460

20   JACKIE

(a)   Jackie is provided with a company car by her employer on 1 May 2020, the day after the car was first registered. The car has a diesel engine, CO_2 emissions of 107 g/km and does not meet the RDE2 standards. The car had a list price of £12,400.

The company had optional accessories costing £1,500 fitted to the car after it was delivered.

During 2020/21 the car was badly damaged in two accidents and Jackie was without the car for two weeks in August and another 3 weeks in October. She was not provided with a replacement car for these periods.

(i)	What is the appropriate car benefit percentage for this car?	%
(ii)	What is the cost of the car to use in the taxable benefit calculation?	£
(iii)	Jackie is not taxed on her car benefit for the 5 weeks during 2020/21 when the car is unavailable.	True/False
(iv)	What is Jackie's taxable car benefit for 2020/21?	

(b) **Are the following statements true or false when determining that a car is to be treated as a pool car and give rise to no taxable benefit?**

Tick the appropriate box for each statement.

	True	False
A pool car can be used exclusively by one employee		
A pool car is normally garaged at the company premises		
A pool car should only be used for business travel		

TAXABLE BENEFITS – ALL EXCLUDING CARS

Key answer tips

Task 3 in the sample assessment consists of several questions, each of which tests knowledge of a different taxable or exempt benefit.

21   YOSEF

(a)   On 2 June 2020 Yosef was provided by his employer with a laptop computer costing £750 for private use.

What is the taxable benefit for 2020/21?

> [ ]

(b)   On 4 August 2020 Ian was provided by his employer with a van with a list price of £12,000 for private use. The van has zero CO_2 emissions. Ian is not provided with any private fuel.

What is the taxable benefit for 2020/21?

> [ ]

(c)   On 6 April 2020 Siti left her employment. She took up the offer of purchasing a camera for £200 which she had been lent by her employer several years previously.

This camera cost the company £500 and up to the end of 2020/21 Siti had been taxed on taxable benefits totalling £350.

The camera was worth £250 at 6 April 2020.

What is Siti's taxable benefit for 2020/21?

> [ ]

(d) Angel was provided with job related accommodation throughout 2020/21.

This house cost her employers £125,000 in June 2018. The house has an annual value of £2,250. Angel's employer provided her with furniture at a cost of £10,000 and paid for the electricity bill which cost £1,200. Angel earns a salary of £22,000 for 2020/21

What is Angel's taxable benefit for the provision of the accommodation for 2020/21?

```
┌─────────────────────────┐
│                         │
└─────────────────────────┘
```

(e) Since 1 August 2020, Esme has lived in a house provided by her employer.

This house cost her employers £175,000 in June 2013. The house has an annual value of £3,250 and Esme contributes £100 per month towards the cost of the benefit. The property had a market value of £228,000 when Esme moved in.

What is Esme's taxable benefit for 2020/21?

```
┌─────────────────────────┐
│                         │
└─────────────────────────┘
```

22 LOACH

(a) On 6 December 2020, Loach was provided with a company loan of £7,000 on which he pays interest at 1.4% per annum.

What is the taxable benefit for 2020/21?

```
┌─────────────────────────┐
│                         │
└─────────────────────────┘
```

(b) Swift plc purchased a property for £100,000 in December 2014. In May 2015 the company spent £30,000 on an extension to the property.

On 1 November 2019 an employee, Margarita, occupied the property. The market value of the property on 1 November 2019 was £220,000.

What is the additional 'expensive accommodation' benefit to be taxed on Margarita for 2020/21?

A   £1,238

B   £563

C   £3,263

D   £516

(c) **Which of the following situations would be treated as being job related such that no accommodation benefit arises?**

Assume that there are no special security considerations.

Tick the appropriate box for each option.

	Job related	Not job related
Accommodation provided for a priest		
Accommodation provided for a tutor at a boarding school		
Accommodation provided for directors to enable them to get to work more easily		

(d) Eve was provided with a flat (which was not job related) by her employer.

The flat has an annual value of £6,000 and Eve's employer pays rent of £450 per month. Eve pays £100 per month towards the private use of the flat.

What is Eve's taxable benefit for 2020/21?

(e) **Read the following statements and tick the appropriate box to indicate whether they are true or false.**

	True	False
Furniture provided by an employer is taxed at 25% of the market value per annum		
Provision of workplace child care is an exempt benefit		
A loan of £12,000 provided to an employee in order that they can buy items wholly, exclusively and necessarily for their employment is exempt from income tax		
Reimbursement of expenses for home to work travel is not a taxable benefit for the employee		
Provision of eye tests and spectacles for VDU use is an exempt benefit for an employee		

23 BHARAT

(a) On 6 October 2020, Bharat was provided with a loan of a home cinema system worth £3,600 by his employer. The cinema system is only used for private purposes.

What is the taxable benefit for 2020/21?

(b) **When accommodation is purchased by an employer for use by an employee, the market value of the property will be used to calculate the additional benefit if the employee moves in more than how many years after the property was purchased?**

(c) Which of the following situations would be treated as being job related such that no accommodation benefit arises?

Tick the appropriate box for each option.

	Job related	Not job related
Accommodation provided for a matron at a boarding school		
Accommodation provided for the Prime Minister		
Accommodation provided for a sales director so that he may entertain prospective customers. There are no special security considerations.		

(d) Sybil was provided with a flat (which is not job related) by her employer.

The flat has an annual value of £5,600 and Sybil's employer pays rent of £420 per month. Sybil pays £80 per month towards the private use of the flat.

What is Sybil's taxable benefit for 2020/21?

>

(e) Which of the following statements is/are correct for accommodation which is not job related?

(i)   Furniture provided by an employer is an exempt benefit

(ii) Furniture provided by an employer is taxed on the cost to the employer in the year of purchase

(iii) Accommodation expenses paid for by the employer are taxed on the employee at an amount equal to the cost to the employer

(iv) If the employer provides furniture with accommodation it is an additional benefit to the employee

A   (ii) and (iii)

B   (i) and (iii)

C   (iii) and (iv)

D   (iv) only

24 NIKITA

(a) On 6 October 2020, Nikita was provided with a company loan of £28,000 on which she pays interest at 1.0% per annum.

What is the taxable benefit for 2020/21?

>

(b) Percy's employer provides him with a van for private use. The van has a market value of £20,000 and CO_2 emissions of 130 g/km. Percy is not provided with any fuel for private use. Percy has the use of the van throughout 2020/21.

What is the taxable benefit for 2020/21?

>

(c) Molly was provided with a house (which is not job related) by her employer for the whole of 2020/21.

The house has an annual value of £5,000 and cost Molly's employer £150,000 in September 2019. The house contains furniture costing £40,000. Heating bills of £750 per year are paid by her employer. Molly pays £200 per month towards the private use of the house.

What is Molly's taxable benefit for 2020/21?

(d) **Which two of the following statements are correct?**

(i) Assets lent to an employee are taxed at 20% per annum of the market value when first made available to the employee.

(ii) Assets lent to an employee are taxed at 2.25% per annum of the market value when first made available to the employee.

(iii) The car benefit for a pool car is limited to 10% of the total benefit.

(iv) Loan benefits can be reduced by interest payments made by the employee.

A (i) and (iii)

B (ii) and (iii)

C (iii) and (iv)

D (i) and (iv)

25 GIBBS

(a) Gibbs is provided with accommodation by his employer, Tallmark plc.

The property cost Tallmark plc £250,000 in May 2017 and the company spent £45,000 on improvements in June 2020.

The property has an annual value of £6,500 and Gibbs pays rent of £150 per month to Tallmark plc. The property had a market value of £265,000 when Gibbs moved in on 20 December 2017.

What is the taxable benefit for 2020/21 for the provision of the accommodation?

(b) Diego is provided with a house by his employer.

The property was furnished by his employer at a cost of £20,000. The employer also paid for regular gardening and cleaning at the property which cost a total of £2,100 for 2020/21.

In addition the employer spent £5,600 during 2020/21 on extending the garage.

What is the taxable benefit for the furniture and the expenses incurred?

(c) During 2019/20 Bismah receives a £100 payment under her employer's staff suggestion scheme in respect of a proposal she made that reduced the costs incurred by the business.

Her employer also pays her home telephone bills of £400 even though Betsy has no business use of the telephone.

What is Bismah's total taxable benefit in respect of the payment under the staff suggestion scheme and the telephone bills?

[   ]

(d) Bismah's employer moved to larger premises which have a staff canteen available to all staff.

Bismah is entitled to subsidised meals in the canteen for which she paid £1 per day for 250 days. The meals cost her employer £480 to provide.

What is Bismah's taxable benefit in respect of the canteen?

[   ]

26 PERDITA

(a) **Perdita has asked you to advise her of which of the following benefits are exempt.**

Tick one box on each line.

	Exempt	Not exempt
One mobile telephone per employee		
Use of a pool car		
Use of a van for a fortnight's camping holiday. There is no other private use.		
Provision of a car parking space in a multi-storey car park near the place of work	/	
Provision of bicycles for staff who have worked for the company for at least seven years		
A birthday present for an employee, which cost the employer £40.		
Provision of an interest free loan of £9,000 made on 6 April 2020 and written off on 5 April 2021:		
– provision of loan		
– write off of loan		

(b) Althea's employer made an interest-free loan to her of £16,000 on 1 April 2020. On 30 June 2020 Althea repaid £4,000 of the loan.

What is Althea's loan benefit for 2020/21 using the average method of assessment?

27 JOEY

Complete the following sentences, all of which relate to benefits.

(a) The taxable benefit for a pool car with CO_2 emissions of 122 g/km and a list price of £15,000 which runs on diesel and doesn't meet the RDE2 standards is £...............................

(b) The maximum capital contribution that can be deducted from the list price when calculating a car benefit is £...........................

(c) A van with a list price of £14,000 and zero CO_2 emissions was made available to an employee for the whole of 2020/21. The taxable benefit is £...........................

28 HF LTD

(a) HF Ltd is considering whether to provide its employees with fitness facilities.

They have to decide between the following options:

(i) Building a gym at the company premises which will only be open to employees. The annual running costs of the gym would be £450 per employee.

(ii) Paying annual subscriptions at health clubs and gyms near to the employees' homes. Subscriptions up to £450 would be paid for each employee.

Which of these options results in the lower taxable benefit for individual employees?

A (i)

B (ii)

C Neither, because they both produce the same result.

(b) **Long service awards up to £..................... per year of service are tax free.**

(c) **Long service awards for .... years or more of service are tax free.**

(d) **A long service award will only be exempt provided no similar payment has been made within the last ....years**

29 JADEJA PLC

Jadeja plc provides the following benefits to its employees. Which of them are exempt, partly exempt or taxable for the recipient?

Tick one box on each line.

	Exempt	Not exempt	Partly exempt
Free annual health screening which costs the employer £350 per head.			
An annual staff party which costs £220 per head			
Payments of £7 per night for personal expenses when employees have to stay away from home elsewhere in the UK			
Removal expenses of £12,000 paid to an employee who had to relocate to a new town when she was promoted			
A smart phone issued to all staff of manager grade			

30   DHONI LTD

Which of the following benefits provided to employees of Dhoni Ltd are exempt or taxable, for the recipient?

Tick one box on each line.

	Exempt	Taxable
Payment of £800 fees for office employees attending computer skills courses		
A training course entitled 'What you need to know about being self-employed' for an employee who is shortly to be made redundant, which cost Dhoni Ltd £500.		
Long service awards of £500 cash for employees completing 20 years' service		
Private medical insurance for employees who work only in the UK		
A payment of £500 to an employee in accordance with the rules of the staff suggestion scheme.		
Free eye tests for all staff working with computers		

INCOME FROM PROPERTY

Key answer tips

Income from property is covered in task 5 of the sample assessment. The task consists of three separate questions, each of which tests various aspects of this area. Some of the questions in this section of the kit are multi part, whilst others are shorter questions which give practice on the individual parts likely to be tested in a task on this area of taxation.

31 GIORGIS

Are the following statements true or false?

Tick one box on each line.

	True	False
Giorgis has bought a house which he intends to let furnished. The initial cost of providing the furniture will be an allowable cost when calculating taxable property income		
Income from property is always taxed on the cash basis unless the taxpayer elects to use the accruals basis		
When calculating an individual's property income any costs of improving the property are not allowable		
Property losses from furnished lettings can be deducted from profits on unfurnished lettings		
Property losses can be offset against an individual's total income in the tax year		
Property expenses incurred when the property is empty cannot be deducted from property income, even if the property is available to let		

32 HOWARD

(a) **Howard elects to use the accruals basis in respect of an unfurnished flat. Which of the following expenses would not be deductible from rental income?**

(i)   Water rates

(ii)   Legal fees in respect of the purchase of the property

(iii)   Installation of a new free-standing gas fire

(iv)   Advertising for a new tenant

A   (i) and (ii)

B   (ii), (iii) and (iv)

C   (i) and (iv)

D   (ii) and (iii) only

(b) Howard drives 11,000 miles during the tax year 2020/21 in managing his property business. He incurs motor expenses of £6,100 in respect of this mileage, which was all paid during the tax year 2020/21.

How much is deductible from his property income in respect of the above mileage in the tax year 2020/21?

33 GOOGOOSH

Googoosh has two properties, details of which are:

One bedroom flat:

1   This furnished flat has been occupied by the same tenants for several years, and the rent was £500 per month during 2019, payable on the first of the month. On 1 January 2020 the rent was increased to £525 per month, still payable on the first day of each month.

2   Googoosh incurred insurance costs of £100 per month which she always pays on the 11th of the month. Her insurance costs rose to £120 from 1 December 2020. She also paid for various repairs totalling £450.

3   Googoosh purchased a new bed for the property for £800. A bed similar to the old bed would have cost £620. Googoosh was able to sell the old bed for £130.

Four bedroom house:

4   This unfurnished house is rented out for £480 per month, payable on the 10th of the month, but was empty until 1 November 2020 when a family moved in on a twelve month lease.

5   Googoosh paid for a gardener to maintain the large garden at a cost of £20 per month from 1 November 2020.   The gardener is paid at the end of each month.

Calculate the profit or loss made on each property using the following table.

	One bedroom flat £	Four bedroom house £
Income:		
Expenses:		

34   SUNITA

Sunita has two properties, details of which are:

Three bedroom house:

1   This unfurnished house is rented out for £1,000 per month. The property was occupied until 1 September 2020 when the tenants suddenly moved out, owing the rent for August. Sunita knows she will not recover this rent. The property was let again from 1 December 2020 to another family. The rent is received on the first of each month.

2   The only expense payable by Sunita in respect of the house was 5% commission to the agent on rent received. This was deducted from each monthly rent payment.

Two bedroom flat:

3   This furnished flat is rented out for £600 per month. The property was occupied by Sunita during April 2020. She then started looking for a tenant, but the property was unoccupied until 1 July when a couple moved in on a twelve-month lease. The rent was received on the 8th of each month.

4   Sunita incurred letting agency fees of £950 and insurance costs of £400 for 2020/21. Both were paid and payable during the tax year.

5   In May 2020, Sunita purchased new leather lounge furniture for the property for £2,000 and dining furniture for £1,200. Lounge furniture similar to the old furniture could have been purchased for £1,100. Sunita sold the old lounge furniture for £180. The property did not have any dining furniture prior to the purchase in May.

Calculate the profit or loss made on each property using the following table and assuming that Sunita elects to be taxed on the accruals basis.

	Three bedroom house £	Two bedroom flat £
Income:		
Expenses:		

35   WILL

Will has three properties, details of which are:

Two bedroom cottage:

1   This furnished cottage is rented out for £500 per month. All rent was received during the tax year.

2   Will pays gardeners fees of £50 a month and cleaners bills of £70 a month. He also paid for repairs costing £400. All amounts were paid during the tax year, except for the last month's cleaner's fees.

3   Will sold the dining furniture in the cottage for £100 in June 2020. He then purchased replacement furniture for £600. It would have cost £1,300 to buy replacement furniture of a quality similar to the items sold.

One bedroom flat:

4   This furnished flat is rented out for £3,600 per year. The property was unoccupied until 1 July 2020. Rent is paid monthly in arrears.

5   Will paid water rates of £500 and insurance of £500 in respect of the flat for 2020/21 in March 2021.

Three bedroom house:

6   This unfurnished house is rented for £4,320 a year. One month's rent was not received until 15 April 2021.

7   Will paid insurance of £1,000 for the year ended 30 September 2020 on 1 October 2019. This went up to £1,200 for the year ended 30 September 2021 and this amount was paid on 1 October 2020.

Calculate the profit or loss made on each property using the following table.

	Two bedroom cottage £	One bedroom flat £	Three bedroom house £
Income:			
Expenses:			

36   EDWARD

Edward has two properties, details of which are:

Four bedroom house:

1   This unfurnished house is rented out for £7,200 per annum, payable on the first of the month. The property was occupied until 28 February 2021 when the tenants suddenly moved out, without paying the rent for February. Edward moved in for the month of March before the property was let again from 1 April 2021 to another family.

2   The only expenses payable by Edward in respect of the house were £100 advertising fee and £700 on council tax bills. Both expenses were paid during 2020/21.

Two bedroom bungalow:

3   This furnished bungalow is rented out for £550 per month, receivable on the 6th of the month. The property was unoccupied until 6 October 2020.

4   Edward paid council tax bills of £1,100 for the bungalow in respect of 2020/21. He also paid for repairs to the property costing £150.

5   Edward purchased a new sofa for the property for £2,100. A sofa similar to the old one would have cost £900. Edward sold the old sofa for £220.

Calculate the profit or loss made on each property using the following table.

	Four bedroom house £	Two bedroom bungalow £
Income		
Expenses:		

37   REBECCA

Rebecca owns three properties: 15 Olden Way, 29 Harrow Crescent and 42 Long Close. All three properties are let on a furnished basis.

1   15 Olden Way: this property was bought in December 2014.

The rent is £600 per month, payable on the 20th of the month, and the property was occupied throughout the whole of 2020/21.

In May 2020 Rebecca purchased bedroom furniture at a cost of £2,200. She sold the old furniture for £40. Furniture of a similar quality to the old furniture would have cost £1,500.

2   29 Harrow Crescent: this property was bought in June 2017.

The rent is £500 per month, payable on the first of the month. The property was occupied until 30 June 2020 when the tenants moved out. The new tenants moved in on 1 January 2021.

3   42 Long Close: this property was bought on 1 August 2020.

When Rebecca bought the property it was unfurnished, so she spent £3,000 on furniture before the first tenants moved in on 1 November 2020.

The monthly rental is £750.

Expenses for the three properties are:

	15 Olden Way	29 Harrow Crescent	42 Long Close
	£	£	£
Insurance:			
12 months to 31 December 2020 – paid 1 Jan 2020	150	120	
12 months to 31 December 2021 – paid 1 Jan 2021	180	140	
12 months to 31 July 2021 – paid 1 August 2020			160
Water rates – paid and payable re 2020/21	80	100	85

Calculate the profit or loss made on each property using the following table and assuming that Rebecca elects to be taxed on the accruals basis.

	15 Olden Way £	29 Harrow Crescent £	42 Long Close £
Income			
Expenses:			

38 ROSALIE

(a) Rosalie rents out a number of properties and her gross rents for the year are £163,000. In respect of one of her houses, she paid insurance on 1 July 2019 of £1,800 for the year ended 30 June 2020 and £2,160 on the 1 July 2020 for the year ended 30 June 2021.

What is her allowable expense against her property income in respect of this insurance?

[   ]

(b) **Which one of the following statements is incorrect when using the accruals basis to calculate taxable property income?**

A   The cost of replacing furniture with items of a similar quality is allowable expenditure

B   The cost of furnishing a newly acquired property is allowable expenditure

C   Any irrecoverable debts are allowable expenditure when calculating property income

D   Individuals calculate their property income for the tax year

(c) **True or false:**

Losses made on renting out a property can only be offset against property profits.

(d) **True or false:**

Any property losses which cannot be offset in the year they are incurred cannot be carried forward.

39 PROPERTY ALLOWANCE

Are the following statements true or false?

Tick one box on each line.

	True	False
The property allowance is always automatically applied, although the taxpayer can elect not to claim it		
When a taxpayer has rental income of less than £1,000, they do not have to disclose the income to HMRC		
A taxpayer with gross rental income of more than £1,000 and expenses of less than £1,000 should always claim the property allowance		
The time limit for elections with respect to the property allowance for the tax year 2020/21 is 31 January 2023		

INVESTMENT INCOME

Key answer tips

Investment income is covered in task 4 of the sample assessment. The task consists of questions about three separate individuals, and each tests various aspects of this area. Some of the questions in this section of the kit are multi part, whilst others are shorter questions which give practice on the individual parts likely to be tested in a task on this area of taxation.

40 SOPHIE

(a) In 2020/21 Sophie has dividend income of £4,700. £500 of this income falls into Sophie's higher rate band and the remainder falls into her additional rate band.

What is Sophie's income tax liability in respect of her dividend income in whole pounds?

(b) In 2020/21 Serena has savings income of £4,300. £2,100 of this income falls into Serena's basic rate band and the remainder falls into her higher rate band.

What is Serena's income tax liability in respect of her savings income in whole pounds?

41 RAVI

In 2020/21 Ravi has trading profits of £22,000. The only other income he received during the year is the following investment income which was paid directly into his bank account:

Source of income	Amount
Interest from bank account	£250
Dividends from a stocks and shares ISA	£3,200
Dividends from Xi Plc	£14,000
Interest from building society account	£2,200

Calculate the tax payable by Ravi on his investment income by completing the table below. Show the tax payable in whole pounds.

	£
Tax payable on savings income	
Tax payable on dividend income	
Total tax due on investment income	

42 CASTILAS

(a) Castilas' only income for 2020/21 is dividend income of £18,000.

How will the excess of this dividend income over his personal allowance be taxed?

A The first £2,000 at 0% and the balance at 7.5%

B All at 7.5%

C The first £2,000 at 0% and the balance at 32.5%

D All at 32.5%

(b) In the tax year 2020/21 Ramos received a dividend of £7,600. His other taxable income, after personal allowances, totalled £26,300.

What is the income tax payable by Ramos on these dividends in the tax year 2020/21 to the nearest pound?

[   ]

(c) Hannah received bank interest of £8,900 in the tax year 2020/21. Her other taxable income, after any available personal allowance, totalled £116,200.

What is the total income tax payable on this interest by Hannah in whole pounds?

[   ]

43 MARLON

(a) In 2020/21 Marlon has dividend income of £3,300. £1,500 of this income is covered by Marlon's personal allowance and the remainder falls into his basic rate band.

What is Marlon's income tax liability in respect of his dividend income in whole pounds?

[   ]

(b) In 2020/21 Dean has savings income of £8,300. All of this income falls into Dean's higher rate band and Dean has no dividend income.

What is Dean's income tax liability in respect of his savings income in whole pounds?

44 KIRA

Kira has received cash from the following sources.

For each source tick Yes if it is chargeable to income tax and tick No if it is not.

	Yes	No
Profit on disposal of an asset		
Rental profits		
Tips earned whilst working in a bar		
Damages for injury at work		

45 GINNY

Place the following types of investment income in the appropriate column in the table below:

- Interest from NS&I Savings Certificates
- Interest from building society accounts
- Interest from bank accounts
- Interest from Individual Savings Accounts (ISAs)
- NS&I bank interest
- Interest from Gilts (Government stocks)

Exempt from income tax	Taxable

46 TARAN

(a) **Complete the following sentence.**

In 2020/21 the maximum amount that Taran (aged 42) can invest in an ISA is £...........................

(b) **Is the following statement true?**

Dividends received from an ISA are always exempt from tax.

(c) **Is the following statement true?**

When shares held in an ISA are sold, the chargeable gain is exempt.

47   HUANG

(a)   In 2020/21 Huang has savings income of £3,700. £2,100 of this income falls into Huang's higher rate band and the remainder falls into his additional rate band.

What is Huang's income tax liability in respect of his savings income to the nearest pound?

[   ]

(b)   In 2020/21 Michelle has dividend income of £2,600. All of this income falls into Michelle's higher rate band

What is Michelle's income tax liability in respect of her dividend income to the nearest pound?

[   ]

COMPUTATION OF TAXABLE INCOME AND OTHER MATTERS

Key answer tips

The questions in this section bring together much of what has been covered in previous questions. The topics included are total employment income, employment expenses, pension contributions, total taxable income and employment versus self-employment.

48   JESSICA

Jessica provides you with the following information:

(i)   Her annual salary for the twelve months to 30 April 2020 was £36,300.

(ii)   Her annual salary for the twelve months to 30 April 2021 was £20,000.

Her salary is paid in equal monthly instalments on the last day of the month.

(iii)   She received a bonus of £2,300 on 1 May 2020 based on the company's accounting profit for the year ended 30 April 2020.

(iv)   She received a bonus of £1,300 on 1 May 2021 based on the company's accounting profit for the year ended 30 April 2021.

(v)   She receives commission of 7.5% of her salary each month.

Using this information, answer the following questions.

(a)   **What is the taxable salary for 2020/21?**

[   ]

(b)   **What is the taxable bonus for 2020/21?**

[   ]

(c)   **What is the taxable commission for 2020/21?**

[   ]

49   JANE

Jane is employed by Berrow plc. For the year ended 30 June 2020 she received an annual salary of £18,000 and for the year ended 30 June 2021 her salary was increased to £20,000. Jane received her salary in equal monthly instalments on the last day of each month.

The company pays out bonuses each year which are related to the level of profits in the year ended 30 June. Jane received her bonus of £1,000 for the year ended 30 June 2019 on 14 April 2020. She received £1,050 for the year ended 30 June 2020 which was paid on 17 April 2021.

She also received a commission each year equal to 6% of her annual salary. This was paid monthly together with her salary.

Using this information, calculate the answers to questions (a) and (b) and (c).

(a)   **What is the taxable salary for 2020/21?**

(b)   **What is the taxable bonus in 2020/21?**

(c)   **Calculate the taxable commission in 2020/21.**

50   EFFIE

Effie provides you with the following information.

(i)   Her annual salary for the 12 months to 30 September 2020 was £30,000.

(ii)   Her annual salary for the 12 months to 30 September 2021 was £33,600.

       Her salary is paid in equal monthly instalments on the last day of the month.

(iii) Effie pays an annual contribution of £480 to a registered charity through the payroll giving scheme.

(iv)   Effie also makes a payment of £800 to her local church (also a registered charity) through the gift aid scheme.

(v)   She receives reimbursed expenses of £1,260 during 2020/21. All of these costs were incurred by Effie wholly, exclusively and necessarily in the performance of her duties.

What is Effie's taxable employment income for 2020/21?

51   HUI

Hui provides you with the following information.

His monthly salary, paid on the last day of the month, was £1,300 until 31 December 2020. From 1 January 2021 he received a monthly salary of £1,600.

Hui also receives an annual bonus based on profits which is paid to him on 15 April following the company's year end of 31 December. His bonus for the year ended 31 December 2019 was £1,125, for the year ended 31 December 2020 was £1,200 and for the year ended 31 December 2021 was £1,500.

Using this information, answer the following questions.

(a)   What is Hui's taxable salary for 2020/21?

> [   ]

(b)   What is Hui's taxable bonus for 2020/21?

> [   ]

52   MANINDER

Maninder has given you the following details about her employment income.

(i)   She receives a salary of £25,000 per year.

(ii)   She pays a donation to charity each month of £20 through the payroll giving scheme.

(iii)   She contributes 5% of her salary to her employer's occupational pension scheme.

(iv)   She receives a round sum allowance of £1,000 per month of which 70% is spent on business travel and subsistence and 30% on entertaining clients.

What is Maninder's taxable employment income?

> [   ]

53   SALLY

(a)   Sally uses her own car for business travel.

During 2020/21 she travelled 20,000 business miles for which she was paid 25p per mile by her employer.

The impact of this is:

A   She will have taxable employment income of £2,000

B   She will have taxable employment income of £4,000

C   She will claim an allowable expense of £2,000

D   She will claim an allowable expense of £4,000

(b)   Ruth is a member of an occupational pension scheme to which she contributes 5% of her salary. Her employer also makes a contribution equal to 5% of her salary.

For 2020/21 her salary was £45,000.

Which ONE of the following statements is correct?

A   Her contribution is £2,250, which is a tax allowable deduction from her gross salary

B   Both the employee's and employer's contributions are tax allowable deductions from her gross salary

C   Her income tax payable will be reduced by £2,250

D   Her employer's contributions are a taxable benefit

(c)   Tilly receives a round sum allowance of £5,000 per annum.

Out of this allowance she pays £800 for business travel and £150 for professional subscriptions. The rest is used for client entertaining.

Which ONE of the following statements is correct?

A   She will be taxed on the full £5,000 allowance with no deductions

B   She will be taxed on a net sum of £4,850

C   She will be taxed on a net sum of £4,050

D   She will not be taxed on any of the round sum allowance

(d)   Henry is an employee. He has a personal pension scheme.

Which ONE of the following statements is <u>always</u> true?

A   Henry's employer does not have an occupational pension scheme

B   Henry's employer does have an occupational pension scheme but Henry is not allowed to join it

C   Henry can contribute into his personal pension scheme and into his employer's occupational pension scheme (if there is one) and receive tax relief for both contributions provided his total contributions do not exceed certain limits

D   Henry's employer must pay contributions to Henry's personal pension scheme

54   BERNIE

Read the following statements about pension contributions and tick the relevant box to mark each one as true or false.

	True	False
Bernie cannot contribute to both a personal pension scheme and to his employer's occupational scheme.		
Personal pension scheme payments are made net of 10% tax.		
Relief for occupational pension payments is given by deducting the payments made from gross earnings.		
Gary pays a cheque for £260 to his personal pension scheme. He will obtain tax relief by extending his basic rate band by £260.		
Sobia is currently unemployed and has no earnings. She cannot contribute to a personal pension scheme because she has no relevant earnings.		
Pension contributions made by an employer on behalf of an employee are a taxable benefit.		

55 RON

(a) Ron uses his own car for business travelling.

During 2020/21 he travelled 18,000 business miles for which he was paid 38p per mile by his employer.

What is the tax impact of this?

A He will claim a tax allowable expense of £340

B He will claim a tax allowable expense of £1,260

C He will have a taxable amount of £340

D He will have a taxable amount of £1,260

(b) George has made £400 of donations in 2020/21.

£150 was paid to a registered charity through the payroll giving scheme and the other £250 was paid to a political party.

Can either of these donations be deducted from employment income for tax purposes?

A Both are allowable as a deduction

B Neither of them is allowed as a deduction

C Only the political donation is allowable

D Only the charitable donation is allowable

(c) Fred is a member of an occupational pension scheme to which he contributes 7% of his salary whilst his employer contributes 3%.

For 2020/21 his salary was £31,000.

The impact of this is:

A His basic rate band will be extended by £2,170

B He can deduct £2,170 from his salary as a tax allowable amount

C His basic rate band will be extended by £2,713

D He can deduct £3,100 from his salary as a tax allowable amount

(d) Fill in the blanks in respect of the following:

An individual can obtain tax relief on personal pension contributions on the higher of

(i) £.............................gross or

(ii) ....% of relevant earnings

56   ASIF

(a)   Asif has made £600 of donations in 2020/21.

£120 was paid to a registered charity through the gift aid scheme and the other £480 was paid to a charity through the payroll giving scheme.

Can either of these donations be deducted from employment income for tax purposes?

A   Both are allowable as a deduction

B   Neither of them is allowed as a deduction

C   Only the payroll giving donation is allowable

D   Only the gift aid donation is allowable

(b)   Which of the following statements about pension contributions are incorrect?

(i)   Personal pension contributions are paid net of 20% tax relief.

(ii)   Personal pension contributions reduce taxable income.

(iii)   Personal pension contributions can be made by both employed and self-employed individuals.

(iv)   Occupational pension contributions are deducted from employment income.

(v)   A taxpayer with relevant earnings of £10,000 can make personal pension contributions up to a maximum of £3,600.

A   (i) and (ii)

B   (ii) and (iv)

C   (iii) and (iv)

D   (ii) and (v)

E   (iv) and (v)

(c)   Asif has used his own car for business travel.

In 2020/21 he travelled 20,000 miles of which 6,000 were for home to work travel. His employer has paid him 28p per mile for the 20,000 miles.

The impact of this is:

A   He will have a tax allowable expense of £100

B   He will have a taxable amount of £100

C   He will have a tax allowable expense of £1,400

D   He will have a taxable amount of £1,400

57   ARKAN

Arkan gives you the following information about his income tax for 2020/21.

1   His annual salary was £90,000 until 1 October 2020 when he received a 3% pay rise. He is paid at the end of each month.

2   He has the use of a company car for which the annual taxable benefit is £5,500. He pays for all his own petrol.

3   On 7 April 2020 he received a bonus of £5,000 which related to the sales he had made in the year ended 31 December 2019. On 8 April 2021 he received a bonus of £7,500 which related to the sales he had made in the year ended 31 December 2020.

4   He received a dividend from Jay plc of £11,000 in June 2020.

5   During 2020/21 Arkan received £750 interest from a building society and £400 interest from an ISA

6   He pays 5% of his salary into a personal pension scheme.

Complete the following table to calculate Arkan's taxable income for 2020/21.

You should use whole pounds only. If your answer is zero please include '0'. Do not use brackets or minus signs.

	£
Salary	
Personal pension scheme	
Bonus	
Car benefit	
Dividend	
Building society interest	
Interest from ISA	
Personal allowance	
Taxable income	

58   PHLOX

Phlox gives you the following information about his income tax for 2020/21.

1   His annual pension was £15,000 until 31 December 2020 when it was increased by 2%.

2   He received a dividend from Enterprise plc of £5,000 in June 2020 and a dividend of £900 from shares held in an ISA.

3   During 2020/21 Phlox received £7,500 of interest from a building society and £705 of interest from an NS&I bank account

4   Phlox makes a payment of £400 to Oxfam each year under the gift aid scheme.

5   Phlox sold shares during the year making a gain of £4,150

Complete the following table to calculate Phlox's taxable income for 2020/21.

You should use whole pounds only. If your answer is zero please include '0'. Do not use brackets or minus signs.

	£
Pension	
Dividend from Enterprise plc	
ISA dividend	
Building society interest	
NS&I bank interest	
Gift aid payment	
Gain on shares	
Personal allowance	
Taxable income	

59 ALEXIS

Alexis gives you the following information about her income tax for 2020/21.

1   Her annual salary was £40,000 until 1 September 2020 when she received a pay rise of £2,000 per annum. She is paid on the last day of every month.

2   Alexis receives a commission based on 1% of the sales she has made for the year ended 31 December. This is paid annually to her on the following 1 May. The sales she has made are as follows:

Year ended 31 December 2019	£120,000
Year ended 31 December 2020	£135,000

3   Alexis does not have the use of a company car but is paid a mileage allowance of 35 pence per mile for every business mile. She travelled 14,000 business miles during 2020/21

4   She received a dividend from Ark plc of £1,000 in August 2020.

5   During 2020/21 Alexis received £437 of interest from a building society and £400 of interest from an ISA.

6   She pays 5% of her salary into her employer's pension scheme. Her employer pays an amount equal to 6% of her salary into the scheme.

Complete the following table to calculate Alexis's taxable income for 2020/21.

You should use whole pounds only. If your answer is zero please include '0'. Do not use brackets or minus signs.

	£
Salary	
Commission	
Contribution to employer pension scheme	
Employer's pension contribution	
Mileage allowance – taxable amount	
Mileage allowance – tax allowable expense	
Dividend	
Building society interest	
Interest from ISA	
Personal allowance	
Taxable income	

60 DOMINIC

Dominic has a salary of £54,000 with no other income or tax allowable expenses. He wants to start paying 7% of his salary into a personal pension scheme during 2020/21.

Explain to Dominic how he will get tax relief on his contribution, what effect this will have on his tax liability for 2020/21 and the net after tax cost of making his contribution (i.e. cash paid less any tax saved).

61 EMPLOYMENT STATUS

For each statement, tick either employment or self-employment.

	Employment	Self-employment
Contract for services is for		
Contract of service is for		
A worker providing their own tools to perform the work would indicate		

62 EMPLOYMENT OR SELF-EMPLOYMENT

For each statement, tick either employment or self-employment.

	Employment	Self-employment
Minimal degree of control exercised		
Being personally responsible for poor work		
Provision of sick and holiday pay		
Being able to hire helpers		
Carrying out an engagement for a long period		
Regular payment on a monthly basis		

COMPUTATION OF TAX PAYABLE AND PAYMENT OF TAX

Key answer tips

This area is covered in task 6 of the sample assessment. Students are provided with a blank grid in the assessment into which they must enter the proforma for taxable income and income tax liability.

63   MARYAM

During 2020/21 Maryam earned property income of £48,000. She also received interest from a bank account of £250, interest from an ISA of £300 and dividends of £14,000 from Xy Ltd.

Maryam has a property loss of £600 brought forward from 2019/20 and paid £40 per month in gift aid donations.

Use the table below to calculate Maryam's income tax liability for 2020/21. Show the income and tax liability in whole pounds.

64   LUCIA

During 2020/21 Lucia earned a salary of 40,000. She also received lottery winnings of £10,000, building society interest of £800 and dividends from Zi Ltd of £18,000.

Lucia paid 2% of her salary into her personal pension scheme during the year.

Use the table below to calculate Lucia's income tax liability for 2020/21. Show the income and the tax liability in whole pounds.

65   ROMAN

During 2020/21 Roman received a pension of £23,626, property income of £3,000, savings income of £2,720 and dividends of £6,144.

Use the table below to calculate Roman's income tax liability for 2020/21. Show the income in whole pounds and the tax liability to the nearest pound.

66 RAY

During 2020/21 Ray received employment income of £50,870 and savings income of £3,700. He made a gift aid payment of £400 in May 2020.

Use the table below to calculate Ray's income tax liability for 2020/21. Show the answer in whole pounds.

67   JJ

During 2020/21 JJ received employment income of £148,200, building society interest of £7,150 and dividends of £7,556.

Use the table below to calculate JJ's income tax liability for 2020/21. Show the income in whole pounds and the tax liability to the nearest pound.

68   BILL

During 2020/21 Bill had employment income of £54,600 (PAYE deducted of £9,340) and received building society interest of £3,000.

Use the table below to calculate Bill's income tax payable/repayable for 2020/21. Show your answer in whole pounds.

69   FENFANG

During 2020/21 Fenfang received £70,000 salary (gross amount) and £40,200 of dividends (none from ISAs).

She paid a personal pension scheme contribution of £2,000 and made gift aid payments to charity totalling £160. PAYE of £15,500 was deducted from her salary.

Use the table below to calculate Fenfang's income tax payable for 2020/21. Show the income in whole pounds and the tax liability to the nearest pound.

TAX MINIMISATION

Key answer tips

This area is covered in task 7 in the sample assessment. The questions in this section of the kit give practice on the individual aspects likely to be tested in this area.

70   ARON AND VIKTOR

(a)   Aron and Viktor are married. Aron earns a salary of £160,000 per year whereas Viktor's salary is £20,000. Aron also owns shares generating income of £6,000 year.

To minimise the couple's joint income tax liability Aron should:

A   Transfer all shares into Viktor's name

B   Retain all shares in his own name

C   Transfer a proportion of the shares into Viktor's name

(b)   **Mark the following statements as true or false**

	True	False
Paloma's only income is employment income of £45,000. Paloma can receive savings income of up to a maximum of £500 without having any further income tax liability.		
All taxpayers, regardless of the rate of tax they pay, can receive tax-free dividend income of £2,000 per year.		
Nita has net income of £106,000 a year. To receive a full personal allowance in 2020/21 she must make gift aid donations of £4,800		

71   CRISPIN AND AMANA

(a)   The annual income received by Crispin and his wife Amana is set out below.

	Crispin	Amana
	£	£
Employment	175,000	17,000
Bank interest income	7,800	Nil
Dividend income	11,500	Nil

Crispin and Amana are willing to transfer bank deposits and/or shares to each other in order to adjust the levels of their investment income if it would be tax efficient to do so.

Explain how the couple's investment income should be split between them in order to minimise their total tax liability.

(b) Mark the following statements as true or false

	True	False
Flora is provided with a £9,000 loan by her employer. She has never been lent money by her employer before. In order for this loan to be tax free, the employer must charge interest above 2.25%.		
Dexter's only income is rent received of £12,000. His expenses in relation to this letting are £780. Dexter can receive dividend income of up to a maximum of £3,500 without having any income tax liability.		

72 FREYA

Freya is to be provided with a petrol driven company car on 6 April 2020 (the car will be registered on this date). The car will have CO_2 emissions of 113 g/km and a list price of £17,400.

Freya's employer will pay for the petrol used by Freya for business purposes, of £2,800 per year, and for private purposes, of £1,700 per year.

Freya is a higher rate taxpayer.

(i)	How much income tax will Freya save annually if she contributes **£2,000 towards the capital cost of the car?**	£
(ii)	How much income tax will Freya save annually if she contributes **£600 per year towards the cost of using the car for private purposes?**	£
(iii)	How much income tax will Freya save annually if she contributes **£480 per year towards the cost of the private use petrol?**	£

73   MITCHELL

Mitchell is to be provided with a diesel driven company car on 1 January 2020, when the car was registered. The car will have CO_2 emissions of 116 g/km, a list price of £22,300 and doesn't meet the RDE2 standards.

Mitchell's employer will pay for the fuel used by Mitchell for both business and private purposes. The fuel used for private purposes will cost £1,300 per year.

Mitchell is a basic rate taxpayer.

Identify how the following changes to Mitchell's benefit will affect the income tax charge for the tax year 2020/21. Assume each change is the only adjustment to the information above.

(i)	How much income tax will Mitchell save annually if he contributes **£5,700 towards the capital cost of the car?**	£
(ii)	How much additional income tax will Mitchell pay annually if he has **£185 of accessories added to his car on 6 April 2020?**	£
(iii)	How much income tax would Mitchell save annually if the car had been registered and provided on **6 April 2020 instead of 1 January 2020?**	£

NATIONAL INSURANCE CONTRIBUTIONS

Key answer tips

This area is covered in task 7 in the sample assessment. The questions in this section of the kit give practice on the individual aspects likely to be tested in this area.

74   TING

Are the following statements true or false in connection with class 1 national insurance contributions?

Tick the appropriate box for each statement.

	True	False
Ting has attained state pension age but continues to work part-time earning £20,000 per year. Ting's employer has to pay national insurance contributions in respect of her earnings.		
Bo is 47 years old. He is a self-employed entertainer at children's parties making a profit of £35,000 per year. Bo is required to pay class 1 employee contributions in respect of this profit.		
Michael is 32 years old. In 2020/21 he earned a gross salary of £37,000. He contributed £3,800 to an occupational pension scheme during the year. Michael's total liability to national insurance contributions for 2020/21 is £3,300.00 ((£37,000 – £9,500) x 12%).		

75   JEREMY

(a)   Jeremy is 49 years old. He received the following from his employer in 2020/21.

	£
Salary	31,000
Benefit in respect of low interest loan	800
Pension contributions made by Jeremy's employer	1,800

Jeremy made pension contributions of £2,400 in 2020/21.

What are Jeremy's earnings for the purposes of calculating his class 1 national insurance contributions for 2020/21?

```


```

(b)   Aishah is 71 years old and in receipt of a state pension. She received the following from her employer, Hawk Ltd, in 2020/21.

Salary	42,400
Benefit in respect of accommodation	4,100
Free parking place – cost to Hawk Ltd	2,200
Benefit in respect of company car	3,100

What amount of class 1A national insurance contributions will Hawk Ltd have to pay in respect of Aishah in pounds and pence?

```


```

76   MURRAY

Murray is 35 years old and is employed by Lob Roll Ltd. In 2020/21 Murray received the following from his employer:

	£
Salary	126,000
Benefit in respect of company car and fuel	14,400
Free meals with all of the company's employees in the company's canteen with a value of	3,750

Murray made pension contributions of £27,000 in 2019/20. He also incurred expenses of £4,650 wholly, exclusively and necessarily in the performance of his duties.

Your answers to this question should all be in pounds and pence.

(a)   **What is Murray's liability to class 1 national insurance contributions for 2020/21?**

(b)   **What is Lob Roll Ltd's liability to class 1 national insurance contributions for 2020/21 in respect of Murray?**

(c)   **What is Lob Roll Ltd's liability to class 1A national insurance contributions for 2020/21 in respect of Murray?**

77   LUKA

Luka is 22 years old and is employed by Hounds Ltd. In 2020/21 Liam received a gross salary of £4,800 per month. He also received taxable benefits totalling £8,300. None of the benefits is convertible into cash.

Your answers to this question should all be in whole pounds.

(a)   **What is Luka's liability to class 1 national insurance contributions for 2020/21?**

(b)   **What is Hounds Ltd's liability to class 1 national insurance contributions for 2020/21 in respect of Luka?**

(c)   **What is Hounds Ltd's liability to class 1A national insurance contributions for 2020/21 in respect of Liam?**

78   LEWIS

Lewis is 51 years old and is employed as a director by Auto Ltd. In 2020/21 Lewis received the following from his employer:

	£
Salary	71,000
Bonus	11,000
Benefit in respect of company car and fuel	5,100
Benefit in respect of camera on long term loan	390

Your answers to this question should all be in pounds and pence, and calculated on an annual basis.

(a) What is Lewis' liability to class 1 national insurance contributions for 2020/21?

> [   ]

(b) What is Auto Ltd's liability to class 1 national insurance contributions for 2020/21 in respect of Lewis?

> [   ]

(c) What is Auto Ltd's liability to class 1A national insurance contributions for 2020/21 in respect of Lewis?

> [   ]

79 AMBER

Are the following statements true or false in connection with class 1 national insurance contributions?

Tick the appropriate box for each statement.

	True	False
Amber is 56 years old. In 2020/21 she earned a salary of £40,000. She was also provided with a company car resulting in a taxable benefit of £3,700. Amber's total liability to national insurance contributions for 2020/21 is £4,104.00 ((£40,000 + £3,700 − £9,500) x 12%).		
John is 71 years old and receives a state pension. He is employed by Dory Ltd and was paid a gross salary of £118,000 in 2020/21. John does not have to pay any national insurance contributions in respect of his earnings from Dory Ltd		
Philip is 77 years old and receives a state pension. He works part-time for Innes Ltd and earned £380 per month in 2020/21. Innes Ltd has to pay national insurance contributions in respect of Philip's earnings.		

80 NAOMIE

Naomie is 73 years old and in receipt of a state pension. She is employed by Pirates Ltd. In 2020/21 Naomie received a gross salary of £39,000. She was also provided with a company car resulting in a taxable benefit of £4,150.

Your answers to this question should all be in whole pounds.

(a) What is Naomie's liability to class 1 national insurance contributions for 2020/21?

> [   ]

(b) What is Pirates Ltd's liability to class 1 national insurance contributions for 2020/21 in respect of Naomie?

> [   ]

(c) **What is Pirates Ltd's liability to class 1A national insurance contributions for 2020/21 in respect of Naomie?**

CHARGEABLE GAINS

BASICS OF CAPITAL GAINS TAX

Key answer tips

This area is covered in task 9 in the sample assessment. The task is in three parts. The questions in this section of the kit give practice on the individual parts likely to be tested in this area.

81 CONNECTED PERSONS

For each statement, tick the appropriate box.

	Actual proceeds used	Deemed proceeds used	No gain/ no loss basis
(a) Sister gives an asset to her brother			
(b) Civil partner gives an asset to civil partner			
(c) Tareq sells an asset to his friend for £38,000. He later discovers the asset is worth £45,000.			

82 HARRY AND BEATRIZ

(a) Harry bought a second property as an investment in February 2015 for £155,000. He built a conservatory costing £15,000 and an extension which cost £28,000 during 2016. In 2017 he redecorated the property at a cost of £2,200.

In March 2021 he sold the entire property for £400,000.

What is the gain on this asset?

(b) Beatriz bought an antique set of 6 chairs in August 2017 for £15,000, and then sold two of them in January 2021 for £10,000. The market value of the remaining 4 chairs is £25,000.

In the chargeable gain calculation what is the allowable cost of the two chairs sold?

(c) **True or False:**

Auctioneers fees are never an allowable deduction from sales proceeds.

---

83   SAMANTHA

For each statement, tick the appropriate box.

	Actual proceeds used	Deemed proceeds used	No gain no loss basis
(a) Samantha sells an asset to her colleague for £8,000. She then discovers that it was worth £10,000			
(b) Neil sells an asset to his wife for £10,000 when the market value is £14,000			
(c) Selim gives an asset to his friend.			

84   JAY AND CARLI

(a)   Jay bought a building for £70,000. He spent £10,000 on repairs to the building and sold it for £120,000.

What is the gain on this asset?

[   ]

(b)   Carli bought an asset for £50,000, selling it for £30,000. She paid auctioneer's commission of 4% when she bought the asset and 5% when she sold the asset.

What is the loss on this asset?

[   ]

(c)   True or false:

If shares are bought for £3,000 and sold for proceeds of £5,000 then the gain of £2,000 is not chargeable because the proceeds and cost are both less than £6,000.

85   VICTORIA

Victoria holds a party which is attended by many people including:

Cecil – her husband

Mike – married to Victoria's daughter

Janet – her sister

Alice – Janet's daughter

Tim – her bank manager

Olive – her cousin

How many of these people are connected with Victoria for capital gains purposes?

A   2

B   3

C   4

D   5

86 JOAQUIN

Joaquin bought an asset for £180,000. He spent £10,000 on repairs and £60,000 on improvements. He sold the asset for £300,000.

What is the gain on this asset?

87 ESHE

Eshe made the following capital disposals in 2020/21.

(i) Sold a necklace worth £50,000 to her sister for £40,000. The necklace had cost Eshe £31,400 in June 2009.

(ii) Gave shares in X plc, a quoted trading company, to her wife's brother. The shares cost £16,700 and were worth £9,000 at the time of the gift.

(iii) Sold an antique table which had cost £8,000 to her cousin for £11,000. £11,000 was the price that an antique dealer had offered to Eshe earlier in the year. Later Eshe discovered its value was in fact £12,000.

No other capital disposals were made.

What is the total of Eshe's taxable gains for 2020/21?

88 KAMILAH

(a) Kamilah owned an antique desk which she bought for £25,000. The desk was destroyed in a fire and she received £48,000 in insurance proceeds.

What is the gain/loss (if any) on this asset? ....

(b) Kamilah owned a set of three paintings. She had bought these for £16,500 in total. She sold one of the paintings for £20,000. The remaining two paintings had a total market value of £36,000.

What is the gain/loss (if any) on this asset? ....

89 ALVIN

Alvin bought a 10 acre field in May 2010 for £40,000. In June 2020 he sold 4 acres for £83,000 net of £2,000 selling expenses. The remaining 6 acres were valued at £110,000.

In December 2020 Alvin sold the remaining 6 acres of land for £118,000 which was the gross proceeds before incurring £1,500 selling expenses.

(a) **What is the gain/loss on the disposal in June 2020?**

(b) **What is the gain/loss on the disposal in December 2020?**

90   REYANSH

Reyansh has disposed of the non-wasting chattels below.

Calculate the gain/loss on each.

Asset	Sale proceeds	Cost	Gain/Loss
1	£5,000	£4,000	
2	£10,000	£7,000	
3	£9,000	£3,000	
4	£4,000	£9,000	

91   CHATTELS – MARGINAL GAIN

On which of the following disposals is the gain calculated using the chattel marginal gain rules?

Tick the appropriate box for each disposal.

	Applies	Does not apply
A racehorse bought for £4,000 and sold for £7,500		
A necklace bought for £5,900 plus £200 of auction costs, and given away when its market value was £8,000		
An antique vase bought for £3,000 and sold for £8,200		
A painting bought for £3,000 and sold for £5,900		
Shares bought for £2,100 and sold for £6,900		

92 MATCHING STATEMENTS

Match the following statements to the appropriate asset details.

All of the assets are non-wasting chattels.

Note: you may use a statement more than once.

Asset	Sale proceeds	Cost	Statement
1	£12,000	£18,000	
2	£5,000	£6,000	
3	£8,000	£4,000	
4	£7,000	£6,500	
5	£5,000	£7,000	

Statements:

(i)   Exempt asset disposal

(ii)   Calculate gain as normal

(iii)   Calculate loss as normal

(iv)   Sale proceeds deemed to be £6,000

(v)   Marginal gain restriction applies

93 MARTOK

Martok has disposed of the following assets.

Which are exempt?

	Exempt	Not exempt
A bravery medal he inherited from his father		
A quarter share in a racehorse		
Antique violin sold for £150,000		
His personal computer		
Shares held in an ISA		

TAXATION OF SHARES

Key answer tips

This area is covered in task 10 in the sample assessment. It is an area that will benefit from practising as many questions as possible.

94   **STRINGER LTD**

John bought 8,000 shares in Stringer Ltd for £8 per share in July 2012. In March 2013 he purchased a further 4,000 shares for £9 each and in July 2015 he sold 3,000 shares for £20,000. In May 2019 he received a 1 for 1 bonus issue.

In February 2021 John sold 5,000 shares for £10 per share.

Clearly showing the balance of shares, and their value to carry forward, calculate the gain made on the shares sold in February 2021.

All workings must be shown in your calculations.

95 LULU LTD

Habiba bought 12,000 shares in Lulu Ltd for £4 per share in October 2010. She received a bonus issue of 1 for 12 shares in June 2012 and in April 2016 she sold 3,000 shares for £5 per share.

In January 2021, Habiba sold 8,000 shares for £7 per share.

Clearly showing the balance of shares, and their value to carry forward, calculate the gain made on the shares sold in January 2021.

All workings must be shown in your calculations.

96   GILBERT LTD

Yasmine bought 8,000 shares in Gilbert Ltd for £4 per share in May 2009. She received a bonus issue of 1 for 4 shares in June 2013. In July 2015 she bought an additional 2,000 shares for £8 a share. On 7 September 2020, Yasmine sold 8,000 shares for £65,000 before buying 1,200 shares for £9,600 on 15 September 2020 and 1,000 shares for £10,000 on 18 September 2020.

Clearly showing the balance of shares, and their value, to carry forward calculate the gain made on these shares.

All workings must be shown in your calculations.

97 BELLA

Bella bought 16,000 shares in Nessie Ltd for £6 per share on 9 September 2012. She took advantage of a rights issue of 1 for 8 shares at £4 a share on 14 June 2016. On 14 May 2020, Bella sold 9,000 shares for £11 per share. On 17 May 2020 Bella bought 1,000 shares for £10 per share.

Clearly showing the balance of shares, and their value, to carry forward calculate the gain made on these shares.

All workings must be shown in your calculations.

98 BAJOR PLC

Mohamed has the following transactions in the shares of Bajor plc:

		Number of shares	Cost/proceeds
February 2010	Purchased	2,000	£7,560
July 2012	Bonus issue	1 for 10	
December 2014	Purchased	500	£2,800
April 2016	Rights issue	1 for 5	£2.50 per share
March 2021	Sold	2,500	£17,500

Clearly showing the balance of shares, and their value, to carry forward calculate the gain or loss made on these shares.

All workings must be shown in your calculations.

99   ASPEN LTD

Kerry bought 4,000 shares in Aspen Ltd for £5 per share on 10 November 2016. Aspen Ltd made a bonus issue of 1 for 2 shares on 1 July 2018. On 18 June 2020, Kerry sold 2,000 shares for £6 per share, before buying a further 200 shares for £5.50 a share. On 25 June 2020 Kerry bought 400 shares for £7 per share.

Clearly showing the balance of shares, and their value, to carry forward calculate the gain made on these shares.

All workings must be shown in your calculations.

CAPITAL GAINS TAX EXEMPTIONS, LOSSES, RELIEFS AND TAX PAYABLE

Key answer tips

Calculation of capital gains tax is covered in task 11 in the sample assessment. The questions in this section of the kit give practice on the various areas likely to be tested in the assessment.

100 AGUSTIN

Agustin has an annual salary of £47,000 for 2020/21 and no other income.

He sold a painting in December 2020 for £25,927 which he originally purchased for £8,000 in August 2013. He paid 2% commission on the sale. This was his only capital disposal in 2020/21.

What is JR's capital gains tax payable for 2020/21 to the nearest pound?

101 ANGELA

Angela bought a warehouse as an investment, in May 2015 for £150,000. She spent £29,700 on enhancing the property in April 2017 and sold it for £290,000 in March 2021.

Angela made no other capital disposals in 2020/21.

She has taxable income of £26,445 and made a gift aid payment of £400 in 2020/21.

What is Angela's capital gains tax liability for 2020/21 to the nearest pound?

102 KIESWETTER

(a) **True or false:**

All disposals of animals are exempt from capital gains tax.

(b) **True or false:**

Vintage cars are chargeable assets for CGT purposes.

(c) Kieswetter has chargeable gains for 2020/21 of £20,300 and capital losses of £4,500. He also has capital losses brought forward of £6,700.

What capital loss (if any) can he carry forward to 2021/22?

A £Nil

B £3,200

C £3,500

D £6,700

103 JOANNA

Advise Joanna whether the following statements are true or false.

Tick the appropriate box for each statement.

	True	False
Capital gains are taxed at 10% for all taxpayers.		
If a taxpayer does not use their annual exempt amount in 2019/20 they can bring it forward to use in 2020/21.		
The use of brought forward losses is made after the annual exempt amount.		

104 ALYSHA

Alysha bought a painting in May 2012 for £35,300, selling it in December 2020 for £52,000.

She paid auctioneers commission of 2% when she sold the painting and legal fees of £250 when she bought it.

Alysha has made no other capital disposals in 2020/21 and is a higher rate taxpayer.

She paid her accountant £100 to calculate her capital gains tax liability on this disposal.

What is Alysha's capital gains tax liability for 2020/21 in whole pounds?

105 KEVIN

Kevin has made the following statements. Which of them is/are true?

(i)   Unused personal allowance can be deducted from taxable gains.

(ii)   Current year capital losses are restricted to protect the annual exempt amount.

(iii)   A capital loss made on a disposal to a connected person can only be deducted from gains on disposals to the same connected person.

A   (i) only

B   (ii) only

C   (iii) only

D   (i) and (iii)

106   RASHIDA

In each of the following cases, calculate how much capital loss is available to carry forward to 2021/22

	Capital loss b/f £	Chargeable gain 2020/21 £	Capital loss 2020/21 £	Capital loss c/f £
1	7,560	25,000	11,290	
2	Nil	16,500	21,000	
3	12,900	14,780	8,000	
4	5,200	13,800	Nil	

107   ARLENE

Arlene has a chargeable gain of £31,900 in respect of the disposal of an office held for investment purposes and £4,100 of capital losses for 2020/21. She has £7,200 of her basic rate band unused.

What is her capital gains tax liability for 2020/21 to the nearest pound?

When will this tax be payable?

108   HUEY, DUEY AND LOUIE

The chargeable gains for three taxpayers for 2020/21 are shown in the table below, together with their capital losses brought forward from 2019/20. The gains are before deduction of the annual exempt amount.

Tick the relevant box to show how the losses brought forward will be relieved in 2020/21.

Taxpayer	Net gains 2020/21	Loss 2019/20 b/f	Relieve all loss	Relieve some loss	Relieve no loss
Huey	£21,750	£6,550			
Duey	£10,530	£5,150			
Louie	£15,090	£7,820			

109   TINEKE

Tineke bought a flat on 1 June 2012 for £99,000.

She lived in the house until 31 December 2012 when she moved abroad to work for two years.

Her employer then moved her to another region of England for a secondment when she returned, and this lasted 8 months.

She then moved back into the flat on 1 September 2015 but this was short-lived and she moved out again to live with her boyfriend on 1 December 2015.

She sold the flat on 31 December 2020

Which periods are treated as occupied and which are not?

Occupation	Non-occupation

110   RENATA

Renata bought a house on 1 May 2010 for £50,000.

She lived in the house until 31 December 2013 when she moved in with her sister.

The house remained unoccupied until she sold it on 30 June 2020 for £180,000.

This house is Renata's only property.

Which periods are treated as occupied and which are not?

Occupation	Non-occupation

111 YASMIN

Which of the following absences would be treated as occupation or part occupation of a principal private residence?

Assume that in each case the owner spent all other periods occupying the property, both before and after the absence, unless told otherwise.

	All treated as occupation	Part treated as occupation	Not treated as occupation
(a) Yasmin spent 10 years working abroad.			
(b) George spent 4 years motorcycling around the world.			
(c) The last 4 years of Owen's ownership in which he did not live in the house.			
(d) Ian spent 5 years working elsewhere in the UK			
(e) Irina moved out of her house and spent 2 years living in her boyfriend's house. After they split up she moved back to live with her parents and never moved back to her own house which she sold 5 years later. – for the 2 years living with boyfriend – for the 5 years living with parents			

112 ESME

Esme bought a house on 1 July 2010 for £40,000.

She lived in the house until 30 June 2012 when she left to travel the world for a year.

She then moved back in until 30 June 2015 when she left to move in with her boyfriend.

The house remained unoccupied until she sold it on 30 June 2020 for £285,000.

This house is Esme's only property.

(a)	**The total period of ownership of the house is (in months)**	
(b)	**The period of actual and deemed residence is (in months)**	
(c)	**The chargeable gain on the sale of the house is**	£

113 LYNNETTE

Lynnette sold her private residence making a gain of £360,000.

She had owned the house for 20 years.

The first 8 years she lived in the house and then as her employer relocated his business, she went to work in Scotland. She lived in rented accommodation in Scotland and never returned to her own house.

What is the capital gain on the sale of Lynnette's private residence?

```
┌──────────────────────────────────┐
│                                  │
└──────────────────────────────────┘
```

INHERITANCE TAX

Key answer tips

This area is covered in tasks 12 and 13 in the sample assessment. Some of the questions in this section of the kit are similar in style to those in the sample assessment, whilst others provide practice on the individual parts likely to be tested in this area.

114 TRANSFERS AND EXEMPTIONS (1)

Are the following statements true or false in connection with inheritance tax?

Tick the appropriate box for each statement.

	True	False
The annual exemption can be carried forward for one year but cannot be used until the annual exemption for the current year has been used.		
An exempt transfer may give rise to an inheritance tax liability if the donor dies within seven years.		
Chargeable lifetime transfers may give rise to two separate liabilities to inheritance tax.		

115 SAGAN

Calculate the chargeable amount (i.e. after the deduction of all available exemptions) in respect of each of the following cash gifts which were made on 1 January 2021.

	Gift £	Chargeable amount £
Sagan Sagan's gift was to his son at the time of his wedding. Sagan's only previous gift was £1,650 to a friend on 1 December 2020.	20,000	
Yates Yates made this gift to his uncle. Yates made a gift of £1,100 to his brother on 1 May 2019 and a gift of £1,800 to a friend on 1 July 2020.	4,100	
Porte Porte made this gift to her sister. She had only made two gifts prior to this one, both of which were to her brother. On 1 June 2019 she gave him £220 and on 1 October 2020 she gave him £270.	£8,000	

116 SHARON

In the situations set out below it should be assumed that no annual exemptions are available to the donor.

Tick the appropriate column for each of the gifts.

Lifetime gift	Not exempt	Partly exempt £	Fully exempt £
1 £310 from Sharon to her husband.			
2 A house worth £510,000 to a trust.			
3 £4,000 from Maysoun to her grandson on his wedding day.			

117 TRANSFERS AND EXEMPTIONS (2)

Are the following statements true or false in connection with inheritance tax?

Tick the appropriate box for each statement.

	True	False
The small gifts exemption is £250 per donor per tax year.		
No IHT liability can arise in respect of a gift made more than seven years prior to death.		
An individual who has always lived in America and is not domiciled in the UK may still be liable to pay inheritance tax in the UK.		

118 FROOME

Calculate the chargeable amount (i.e. after the deduction of all available exemptions) in respect of each of the following cash gifts which were made on 1 July 2020.

	Gift £	Chargeable amount £
Froome Froome's gift was to a friend on his wedding day. His only previous gift was £200 to his nephew on 1 March 2020.	8,250	
Mollema Mollema's gift was to a trust. Mollema had not made any gifts prior to 1 July 2020.	32,600	
Cavendish Cavendish made this gift to her niece. Cavendish made a gift of £2,400 to her sister on 1 October 2019 and a gift of £1,900 to her brother on 1 May 2020.	220	

119 ERIC

In the situations set out below it should be assumed that no annual exemptions are available to the donor.

Tick the appropriate column for each of the gifts.

Gift	Not exempt	Partly exempt	Fully exempt
1 A statue worth £830,000 from Eric to a national museum.			
2 A painting worth £11,500 from Gomez to his wife.			
3 £750 from Janine to her son.			

120 TRANSFERS AND EXEMPTIONS (3)

Are the following statements true or false in connection with inheritance tax?

Tick the appropriate box for each statement.

	True	False
Lifetime inheritance tax is charged at 25% on a chargeable lifetime transfer where the donor is paying the tax.		
An individual who is domiciled outside the UK is liable to IHT in respect of their worldwide assets.		
The annual exemption can be carried forward for one year and must be used before the annual exemption for the current year.		

121 ROWENA

(a) **Complete the following sentences using the words on the right.**

Tick the appropriate column for each of the sentences.

	will	will not

1. Rowena is domiciled in the UK. She owns a house situated in Australia worth £720,000.

   The house .... be subject to inheritance tax in the UK when Rowena dies.

	may	will not

2. Ori gave £30,000 to his niece on 1 July 2012. In September 2020 Ori died.

   The gift of £30,000 .... be subject to inheritance tax on Ori's death.

	may	will not

3. Umar gave £2,600 to his brother on 1 July 2018. This was his only gift in 2018/19. Gary died on 1 December 2020.

   The gift of £2,600 .... be subject to inheritance tax on Umar's death.

(b) **Are the following statements true or false in connection with inheritance tax?**

Tick the appropriate column for each of the sentences.

	True	False
Taper relief will reduce a transfer of value made more than three but less than seven years prior to the donor's death.		
Where the donor of a potentially exempt transfer dies within seven years of making the gift, any inheritance tax due is payable by the donee.		

122 FLORENCE

(a) **Complete the following sentences using the words on the right.**

Tick the appropriate column for each of the sentences.

	may	will not

1. Florence gave a house worth £430,000 to her son on 1 October 2014. Florence died on 1 May 2020.

   The house .... be subject to inheritance tax in the UK following the death of Florence.

	would	would not

2. Jemima gave £370,000 to a trust on 1 September 2011. In June 2020 Jemima died.

   Inheritance tax .... have been charged on the gift when it was made.

	will	will not
3 Joshua is domiciled in France. He owns a house situated in the UK worth £675,000. This house .... be subject to inheritance tax in the UK when Joshua dies.		

(b) **Are the following statements true or false in connection with inheritance tax?**

Tick the appropriate column for each of the sentences.

	True	False
The inheritance tax due in respect of the residue of a death estate is paid by the residuary legatee.		
The annual exemption cannot be deducted from the death estate even if there have been no gifts in the year of death.		

123 ADI

Adi made a gift into a trust on 1 November 2017 of £420,000 after deduction of all available exemptions. Adi's gross chargeable transfers in the seven years prior to this gift were £270,000. Adi paid inheritance tax at the time of the gift of £91,250 resulting in a gross gift of £511,250.

On 1 February 2021 Adi died. She had not made any gifts since 1 November 2017.

Calculate the inheritance tax payable at the time of Adi's death in respect of the gift made on 1 November 2017.

All workings must be shown in your calculations.

124 BERNARD

Bernard died on 1 June 2020. His estate was valued at £1,600,000 and included his home, which was valued at £420,000. In his will Bernard left £800,000 to his wife, £100,000 to his son, £20,000 to a UK charity, and the residue of his estate (including his home) to his daughter.

In the seven years prior to his death, Bernard had made gross chargeable transfers of £85,000.

Calculate the inheritance tax payable in respect of Bernard's estate.

All workings must be shown in your calculations.

125 CAMPION

Campion made a gift to his son on 1 January 2016 of £200,000 after deduction of all available exemptions. Campion's gross chargeable transfers in the seven years prior to this gift were £190,000.

On 1 August 2020 Campion died. He had not made any gifts since 1 January 2016.

Calculate the inheritance tax payable at the time of Campion's death in respect of the gift made on 1 January 2016.

All workings must be shown in your calculations.

126 DESDEMONA

Desdemona died on 1 May 2020. She left the whole of her estate, valued at £1,300,000 to her daughter. Her estate did not include any residential property.

Desdemona's husband had died on 1 August 2014. 62% of his nil rate band was used when calculating the inheritance tax due at the time of his death.

In the seven years prior to her death, Desdemona had made gross chargeable transfers of £145,000.

Calculate the inheritance tax payable in respect of Desdemona's estate.

All workings must be shown in your calculations.

127 EMILE

Emile made a gift into a trust on 1 July 2020 of £350,000 after deduction of all available exemptions. It was agreed that any inheritance due would be paid by the trustees of the trust. Prior to this, Emile's only gift had been a gross chargeable transfer of £80,000 to the same trust on 1 May 2019.

Calculate the inheritance tax payable in respect of the gift made by Emile on 1 July 2020.

All workings must be shown in your calculations.

128 FOTHERINGTON

Fotherington died on 1 March 2021. He left the whole of his estate, valued at £1,750,000 to his daughter. His estate included the small flat he lived in, which was valued at £107,000.

On 1 July 2018 Fotherington gave his nephew £45,000 after deduction of all available exemptions. This was Fotherington's only gift during his lifetime.

(a) **Calculate the inheritance tax payable in respect of the gift on 1 July 2018 as a result of Fotherington's death.**

All workings must be shown in your calculations.

(b) **Calculate the inheritance tax payable in respect of Fotherington's estate.**

All workings must be shown in your calculations.

Section 2

ANSWERS TO PRACTICE QUESTIONS

TAXATION AND THE TAX ADVISER

1 PROFESSIONAL CONDUCT IN RELATION TO TAXATION (1)

	True	False
The duty of confidentiality applies to existing clients but not to ex-clients.		✓
There is no obligation to comply with an informal request for information from HM Revenue and Customs.	✓	
A client's tax adviser has the primary responsibility for ensuring that the tax return is correct before it is submitted		✓
Tax evasion is acceptable where the tax being charged is unreasonable.		✓

Tutorial note

The first statement is false because the duty of confidentiality applies to ex-clients as well as to existing clients.

The second statement is true; however, the client should also be advised whether it is actually in their best interests to disclose the information.

The third statement is false because it is the client who has primary responsibility.

The fourth statement is false because tax evasion is never acceptable and is unlawful.

2 PROFESSIONAL CONDUCT IN RELATION TO TAXATION (2)

	True	False
It is acceptable for a tax return to include an estimated figure as opposed to one that is precise.	✓	
It is up to the client to decide whether or not a particular tax-planning strategy is appropriate.	✓	
A notification to HM Revenue and Customs that a tax adviser has ceased to act for a client must include a reason for the adviser's action.		✓
Confidential information must never be disclosed without the client's specific permission.		✓

Tutorial note

The first statement is true – the return may include reasonable estimates where necessary.

The second statement is true – ultimately it is the client's decision as to what planning is appropriate.

The third statement is false because no reason should be given to HM Revenue and Customs due to the need to keep the client's affairs confidential.

The fourth statement is false because information can be disclosed where there is a legal or professional right or duty to disclose the information.

3   PROFESSIONAL CONDUCT IN RELATION TO TAXATION (3)

	True	False
A tax adviser is obliged to provide any information which has been requested by HM Revenue and Customs.		✓
It is acceptable for a tax adviser to provide assistance to a person who has been accused of tax evasion.	✓	
It is essential that a client reviews their tax return before it is submitted, even if the client's affairs are very simple.	✓	
It is up to the client to decide whether or not particular information should be disclosed to HM Revenue and Customs.	✓	

Tutorial note

The first statement is false because a tax adviser should not provide information in response to an informal request, due to the need to preserve confidentiality.

The second statement is true – it is appropriate to act for a client who is rectifying their affairs.

The third statement is true – the taxpayer has primary responsibility to submit correct and complete returns to the best of their knowledge and belief.

The fourth statement is true – the final decision as to whether to disclose any issue must be made by the client.

4   MICROMATTERS LTD

In order to comply with the fundamental principles set out in 'Professional conduct in relation to taxation' a tax adviser must:

– be straightforward and honest in our professional and business relationships;

– respect the confidentiality of information acquired as a result of professional and business relationships and, therefore, not disclose any such information to third parties without proper and specific authority, unless there is a legal or professional right or duty to disclose; and

– comply with relevant laws and regulations and avoid any action that discredits the profession.

It is necessary to consider whether or not the request is valid, how best to comply with it and the consequences of non-compliance. It should be borne in mind that the rules relating to HM Revenue and Customs' powers to obtain information are complex, such that it may be necessary to take specialist advice before responding.

However, reasonable statutory requests for information should be complied with, as, resolving the matter in a prompt manner should help to reduce the costs incurred.

A valid statutory request for information overrides the duty of confidentiality. However, a member must ensure that the confidentiality of information outside the scope of the request is maintained.

As long as we are not precluded from communicating with the client under the terms of the notice, the client should be advised of the notice and kept informed of progress and developments.

Even if the request is invalid, it may make sense to obtain the client's agreement that it should be complied with.

Key answer tips

It is unlikely to be necessary to provide this level of detail in order to obtain the maximum marks in the assessment, however the examiner's feedback does often state that students do not commonly write enough on this task.

Most of this information can be found in the reference material so review this now to see where you can find the relevant material.

Taking a few minutes to brainstorm the areas to cover in your answer using your reference material can help you expand your answer in the exam and maximise your marks.

5   CORA

It is first necessary to establish the facts. We need to know if Cora sold a painting and, if so, the financial details of the sale.

If there is an undeclared chargeable gain, this is an error, which is unlikely to be trivial. It may be that our engagement letter allows us to disclose this to HMRC without specific authorisation from Cora. If it does we should do so.

If not, we must advise Cora to disclose the sale of the painting herself to HM Revenue and Customs immediately. We should advise her of any interest or penalties which may be imposed and the implications for her of not disclosing this information. We would originally do this orally then confirm this in writing.

If Cora refuses to disclose this information, we must cease to act for her. We should inform HM Revenue and Customs that we no longer act for her but we should not provide them with any reasons for our actions.

Finally, we should consider whether or not there is a need to make a suspicious activity report under the anti-money laundering legislation.

Key answer tips

Non-disclosure of a gain is an error. The Helpsheet on Dealing with Errors will help you to answer this question but it is important to apply the information to the scenario in the question.

---

6   TOM

Key answer tips

Even a written question in your exam may have more than one part to it. You must scroll down and ensure you have answered the full question.

By using the reference material properly you should have easily been able to locate the information to answer part (a).

It is important that you can distinguish between three terms in your exam:

1   Tax evasion – the use of illegal methods to reduce a tax liability

2   Tax avoidance – Methods of reducing tax which are legal but not following the intention of legislation

3   Tax planning – tax minimisation methods that are within the letter and the intention of tax legislation.

Part (b) of this question deals with two of these.

(a)   The primary responsibility for information in the returns falls to Tom as the taxpayer. He is responsible for ensuring that the returns filed contain complete and correct information to the best of his knowledge and belief.

The firm's responsibility is to ensure that the return is correct on the basis of the information provided by Tom. We should act in good faith in our dealings with HMRC, and in accordance with the principle of integrity, which requires us to be straightforward and honest in our business dealings.

If we act as a tax agent for Tom, the firm is not required to audit the figures in the books and records provided or verify information provided by either Tom or by a third party. However, we should take care not to be associated with the presentation of facts we know or believe to be incorrect or misleading and not to assert tax positions in a tax filing, which they consider to have no sustainable basis.

(b)   Tax evasion is the use of illegal methods to reduce a tax liability, for example the deliberate omission of income from the return.   The firm should never be knowingly involved in tax evasion, although, of course, it is appropriate to act for a client who is rectifying their affairs.

Tax planning is using the tax legislation legally and as it was intended to minimise the tax liability whilst still paying the correct amount of tax.   Under the Standards for tax planning members 'must not create, encourage or promote tax planning arrangements that (i) set out to achieve results that are contrary to the clear intention of Parliament in enacting relevant legislation and/or (ii) are highly artificial or highly contrived and seek to exploit shortcomings within the relevant legislation'.

7   SOFIA

Key answer tips

The five key standards of tax planning are included in the reference material. These are very relevant for the PLTX syllabus so you must ensure you are happy with where to find them, and how to apply them to a question.

These are the main standards relevant for this scenario but you may pick up marks for discussing some of the others.

The Standards for tax planning should be considered in relation to any tax planning work carried out by the firm. The key standards to consider here appear to be:

- **Client Specific**

  Sofia has stated that this scheme can be used unaltered by many clients. The standards state that tax planning must be specific to the particular client's facts and circumstances. Clients must be alerted to the wider risks and implications of any courses of action.

- **Lawful**

  The interpretation of the law relied on here has not yet been proved in courts. Tax planning should be based on a realistic assessment of the facts and on a credible view of the law.

  The firm should draw any client's attention to where the law is materially uncertain, as is the case here as HMRC is known to take a different view of the law. Members should consider taking further advice appropriate to the risks and circumstances of the particular case, for example, where litigation is likely.

8   ETHICAL RULES

(a)   The answer is D.

The other three statements are correct.

Tutorial note

It is common practice for accountants to prepare tax returns for clients. However, the accountant can only prepare the return based on the information supplied by the client.

The client must always sign the return and the declaration included on the return, to confirm that they have supplied all relevant information.

It is the client's responsibility to submit a completed, signed form as his self-assessment of his own tax position.

(b)   The answer is C.

Tutorial note

An accountant generally needs the client's permission before revealing confidential information.

9   CLIENT ADVICE

(a)   The answer is C.

The other three statements are correct.

Tutorial note

Tax evasion (such as deliberately failing to disclose all of your income) is illegal.

It is tax avoidance that uses legal means to reduce your tax bill.

(b)   The answer is C.

10   AAT STUDENT

(a)   The answer is B.

The other three statements are correct.

Tutorial note

The duty of confidentiality to the client applies in all circumstances to all individuals, except where there is a legal, regulatory or professional duty to disclose (e.g. suspicion of money laundering).

An accountant cannot therefore disclose information to anyone without the client's permission, including the client's spouse or civil partner.

(b)   The answer is D.

Tutorial note

When money laundering is suspected an accountant should report his suspicions. This legal duty overrules the duty of confidentiality.

11   NASHEEN

	True	False
If a husband is ill, it is acceptable to discuss his tax affairs with his wife even if no letter of authorisation exists		✓
Accountants must maintain confidentiality irrespective of the situation		✓

Tutorial note

The first statement is false because the duty of confidentiality to the client applies in all circumstances to all individuals, except where there is a legal, regulatory or professional duty to disclose (e.g. suspicion of money laundering).

An accountant cannot therefore disclose information to anyone without the client's permission, including the client's spouse or civil partner.

The second statement is false because when money laundering is suspected an accountant should report his suspicions. This legal duty overrules the duty of confidentiality.

12   RESIDENCE AND DOMICILE

Are the following statements true or false?

	True	False
An individual is originally domiciled in the country in which he is born		✓
Individuals who are not resident in the UK may still be subject to UK income tax	✓	
An individual is automatically resident in the UK if they own a second home in the UK		✓
An individual whose domicile of origin is France and who has lived in the UK since 2002/03, will be treated as deemed domiciled in the UK	✓	

Tutorial note

The first statement is false because an individual acquires the domicile of his father at birth.

The second statement is true. Individuals who are not resident in the UK are still subject to UK income tax on their UK source income.

*The third statement is false. An individual will be automatically UK resident if their **only** home is in the UK and if they do not meet any of the automatic non UK resident rules first.*

The fourth statement is true. An individual who has been resident in the UK for at least 15 of the last 20 years will be treated as deemed domiciled in the UK.

13   TAX SYSTEMS

Are the following statements true or false?

	True	False
National insurance is a regressive tax	✓	
Inheritance tax is an indirect tax		✓
Proportional taxes take an increasing proportion of income as income rises		✓

Tutorial note

The second statement is false because inheritance tax is a direct tax, i.e. a tax which is imposed directly on the person who is required to pay it.

The third statement is false because a proportional tax is one which takes the same proportion of income as income rises.

14   GERAN

Complete the following sentences using the words/numbers on the right.

	UK income only	Overseas income only	UK and overseas income
			✓

1   Geran is resident in the UK.

He will be subject to UK income tax on his ....

5	8	11
	✓	

2   In 2020/21, Hogan has been in the UK for 175 days.

If Hogan spends a further .... days in the UK he will automatically be UK resident.

16	46	91
		✓

3   Irene works full-time in France.

Irene will be automatically non-UK resident if she is in the UK for less than .... days in the tax year.

Tutorial note

A taxpayer is automatically UK resident if they fail the non-UK tests and they pass one of the three following tests for the tax year:

1   They are in the UK for 183 days or more; or

2   Their only home is in the UK; or

3   They work full time in the UK

Hogan has already spent 175 days in the UK so if he spends another 8 days here in the year.

A taxpayer is automatically non-resident if they pass one of the three following tests for the tax year:

1   They spend less than 16 days in the UK; or

2   They were not resident in any of the three previous years and spend less than 46 days here; or

3   They work full-time overseas and spend less than 91 days in the UK.

As Irene is working full-time in France she will be non-resident if she spends less than 91 days here.

---

15 RESIDENCY STATUS

Explain whether or not the following individuals are resident in the UK in the tax year 2020/21.

1   Kanu has not been resident in the UK in any of the three previous tax years, and has been in the UK for less than 46 days.

Accordingly, he will automatically be treated as **not UK resident** in the tax year 2020/21.

2   Lara is employed full-time in France and has been in the UK for less than 91 days (40 weekends = 80 days) in the tax year 2020/21.

Accordingly, she will automatically be treated as **not UK resident** in the tax year 2020/21.

3   Mavis has only ever lived in the UK, does not work full-time abroad and has been in the UK for more than 16 days in the tax year 2020/21.

Accordingly, she does not satisfy any of the automatic non-UK resident tests.

Her only home is in the UK and therefore she is automatically treated as **UK resident** in the tax year 2020/21.

INCOME TAX

TAXABLE BENEFITS – PROVISION OF CARS

16   SNAPE

(a)   Car benefit percentages

(i)   The answer is 13%.

Tutorial note

The car has CO_2 emissions of between 51 and 54 g/km.

The appropriate percentage is 13% for a petrol car and 17% for a diesel car.

(ii)   The answer is 25%.

CO_2 emissions are rounded down to 110 g/km.

Appropriate percentage = (14% petrol + (110 − 55) × 1/5) = 25%

(iii)   The answer is 29%.

CO_2 emissions are rounded down to 130 g/km.

Appropriate percentage = (14% petrol + (130 − 55) × 1/5) = 29%

(iv)   The answer is 37%.

CO_2 emissions are rounded down to 220 g/km.

Appropriate percentage = (14% petrol + (220 − 55) × 1/5) = 47%

However, the maximum percentage is 37%.

Tutorial note

The cars in (ii) to (iv) have CO_2 emissions in excess of 55 g/km.

The appropriate percentage is therefore calculated in the normal way (i.e. a scale percentage of 14% for petrol cars and 18% for diesel cars, plus 1% for each 5 complete emissions above 55 g/km up to a maximum percentage of 37%).

(b)   Snape's car

(i)   The appropriate car benefit percentage for the car is 33%.

Appropriate percentage for a 134 g/km petrol car is 29% (see (iii) above).

A diesel car has an extra 4% added.

(ii)   The cost of the car to use in the taxable benefit calculation is the list price of £21,995.

(iii)   The standard amount on which the fuel benefit is calculated in 2020/21

= £24,500.

(iv)   Fuel benefit = (£24,500 × 33%) = £8,085

Key answer tips

Note that a mark would be given in part (iv) if you calculated the benefit based on your answers to (i) and (iii).

Tutorial note

Car benefits are calculated as follows:

- *Appropriate percentage × List price × n/12*

- *Where n = number of months the car is available in the tax year.*

The scale percentage is found from the following calculation:

- *14% + (CO$_2$ emissions – 55) × 1/5*

- *CO$_2$ emissions are rounded down to the next number ending in 0 or 5.*

- *Diesel cars attract an extra 4% unless the car is RDE2 compliant.*

- *Maximum scale percentage is 37%.*

Fuel benefit is calculated as follows:

- *Appropriate percentage × £24,500 × n/12*

- *Where n = number of months the benefit is available in the tax year.*

If an employee contributes towards the running costs of the car this is an allowable deduction, but partial contributions towards the cost of private fuel are NOT an allowable deduction.

17 SAM

    (a)   Car benefit percentages

           (i)   The answer = 10%

Tutorial note

For electric/electric hybrid cars (those with emissions up to 50g/km) the drive range of the car must be identified. This car has a range of 39 miles.

The appropriate percentage for a petrol car is 10%, and 14% for a diesel car.

(ii)   The answer = 22%

CO$_2$ emissions are rounded down to 75g/km.

Appropriate percentage = (14% + 4% diesel + (75 – 55) × 1/5) = 22%

(iii)   The answer = 34%

CO$_2$ emissions are rounded down to 135 g/km.

Appropriate percentage = (14% + 4% diesel + (135 – 55) × 1/5) = 34%

(iv)   The answer = 37%

CO$_2$ emissions are rounded down to 200 g/km.

Appropriate percentage = (14% petrol + (200 – 55) × 1/5) = 43%

However, the maximum percentage is 37%.

Tutorial note

Cars (ii), (iii) and (iv) all have CO$_2$ emissions in excess of 55 g/km.

The appropriate percentage is therefore calculated in the normal way (i.e. a percentage of 14% for petrol cars and 18% for diesel cars, plus 1% for each 5 complete emissions above 55 g/km up to a maximum percentage of 37%).

(b)   Sam's car

(i)   What is the appropriate car benefit percentage for this car? (W1) | 35%
(ii)   What is the cost of the car to use in the taxable benefit calculation? (W2) | £27,000
(iii)   What is the amount of car running costs taxed on Sam in 2020/21? | £0

Workings

1   The CO2 emissions are rounded down to 130 g/km.

Appropriate percentage = 14% + 4% diesel + 2% + (130 – 55) × 1/5 = 35%

2   The benefit is based on the original list price.

Tutorial note

An extra 2% must be added to the relevant percentage as the car was registered before 6 April 2020.

An extra 4% must be added to the relevant percentage as the car is a diesel car that does not the RDE2 standards.

The car benefit covers all the running costs of the car except for the provision of private fuel and the services of a chauffeur.

Costs such as repairs, insurance, servicing and road tax are not assessed on the employee.

However, if an employee paid some of these expenses privately they could deduct the amount spent from their taxable car benefit.

---

18   FRODO

(a)   The answer is B.

Tutorial note

Car benefits are calculated based on list price.

(b)   The answer is 26%.

CO_2 emissions are rounded down to 115 g/km.

Appropriate percentage = (14% petrol + (115 – 55) × 1/5) = 26%

Tutorial note

The car has CO_2 emissions in excess of 55 g/km.

The appropriate percentage is therefore calculated in the normal way (i.e. a scale percentage of 14% for petrol cars and 18% for diesel cars, plus 1% for each 5 complete emissions above 55 g/km up to a maximum percentage of 37%).

(c)   The answer is £3,947

Car benefit = £26,000 × 26% × 8/12 (available from 5 August)

less £560 (contribution for private use).

(d)   The answer is £4,247

Fuel benefit = (£24,500 × 26% × 8/12)

Tutorial note

The £70 per month paid in respect of the private use of the car can be deducted from Frodo's car benefit. The total amount deductible is £70 per month for eight months.

The £30 per month partial contribution towards private fuel cannot be deducted from the fuel benefit.

19   BARRY

(a)   Barry's car

(i)	What is the appropriate car benefit percentage for this car? (W1)	34%
(ii)	What is the cost of the car to use in the taxable benefit calculation? (W2)	£22,000
(iii)	What is Barry's taxable car benefit in 2020/21? (W3)	£6,880

Workings

1   CO_2 emissions are rounded down to 125 g/km.

Appropriate percentage = (14% + 4% diesel + 2% + (125 – 55) × 1/5 = 34%

2   Cost of car

= (Manufacturer's list price less capital contribution made by employee)

but note that the maximum capital contribution deduction is £5,000.

= (£27,000 – £5,000 max) = £22,000

3   Car benefit – car available throughout the whole year 2020/21

= (£22,000 × 34%) less (£50 × 12) employee contribution

Tutorial note

For a car first provided before 6 April 2020 an additional 2% is added to the calculation of the appropriate percentage.

The car benefit covers all the running costs of the car except for the provision of private fuel and the services of a chauffeur.

Costs such as repairs, insurance, servicing and road tax are not assessed on the employee.

However, if an employee paid some of these expenses privately they could deduct the amount spent from their taxable car benefit.

(b)   The answer is B.

Working

Fuel benefit = (£24,500 × 24% × 7/12) = £3,430

Tutorial note

The fuel benefit applies because Crouch receives private fuel and does not reimburse his employer the whole cost. Partial contributions towards private fuel are ignored.

The fuel benefit is based on a fixed figure of £24,500 in 2020/21.

The benefit is time apportioned because Crouch only has the car and fuel for 7 months during the tax year from 1 September 2020.

20   JACKIE

(a)   Car benefit

(i)	What is the appropriate car benefit percentage for this car? (W1)	28 %
(ii)	What is the cost of the car to use in the taxable benefit calculation? (W2)	£13,900
(iii)	Jackie is not taxed on her car benefit for the 5 weeks during 2019/20 when the car is unavailable.	False
(iv)	What is Jackie's taxable car benefit for 2019/20? (W3)	£3,568

Workings

1   CO_2 emissions are rounded down to 105 g/km.

Appropriate percentage = (14% + 4% diesel + (105 – 55) × 1/5) = 28%

2   Cost of car = (£12,400 + £1,500 accessories) = £13,900

3   Car benefit = (£13,900 × 28% × 11/12)

Tutorial note

The cost of the car to use in the taxable benefit calculation is the manufacturer's list price plus the cost of accessories purchased with the car, and those added at a later date (unless the accessory cost less than £100).

For the car benefit to be reduced, it must be unavailable for at least 30 consecutive days. Temporary non-availability of less than 30 days is ignored.

Since the car was first provided on 1 May 2020, the benefit only applies for 11 months.

(b)   Pool car

	True	False
A pool car can be used exclusively by one employee		✓
A pool car is normally garaged at the company premises	✓	
A pool car should only be used for business travel	✓	

Tutorial note

There is no benefit where there is provision of a company car (and associated services) which is a 'pool' car.

A pool car is one which is not exclusively used by any one employee, and which is not available for travel from home to work, being garaged at company premises, and is only used for business travel.

TAXABLE BENEFITS – ALL EXCLUDING CARS

21   YOSEF

(a)   The answer is £125.

Working

Use of asset benefit = (£750 × 20% × 10/12) = £125

Tutorial note

The benefit for use of a company asset such as a computer is 20% of the market value of the asset when first made available to the employee.

Yosef has only had use of the laptop for 10 months in the tax year 2020/21, therefore the benefit must be time apportioned.

(b)   The answer is £1,861.

Working

Use of asset benefit = ((£3,490 × 80%) × 8/12) = £1,861

Tutorial note

The benefit for use of a zero emission van is 80% of the basic van benefit.

Ian has only had use of the van for 8 months in the tax year 2020/21, therefore the benefit must be time apportioned.

(c)   The answer is £50.

Gift of asset after previous use of asset benefit = Higher of

(i)   (£250 – £200) = £50, or

(ii)   (£500 – £350 – £200) = £Nil

Tutorial note

When an asset previously used by an employee is sold or given to them the taxable benefit is calculated as follows.

Higher of:

(i)   *Market value of asset at date of transfer to employee less price paid by employee*

(ii)   *Original market value when first supplied as a benefit less amounts taxed as a benefit to date less price paid by employee.*

(d)   The answer is £2,200.

Working	£
Ancillary benefits:	
Use of furniture (£10,000 × 20%)	2,000
Electricity bill	1,200
	3,200
Restricted to 10% of net earnings as job related (£22,000 × 20%)	2,200

Tutorial note

There is no basic charge or expensive accommodation benefit if the accommodation is job related.

(e)   The answer is £3,662.

Working	£
Annual value	3,250
Additional charge for 'expensive' accommodation:	
(£228,000 – £75,000) × 2.25% (Note)	3,443
	6,693
Time apportion – from 1 August 2020 to 5 April 2021 (£6,693 × 8/12)	4,462
Less: Rent paid by Esme (£100 × 8 months)	(800)
Taxable benefit – 2020/21	3,662

Tutorial note

The house was purchased by Esme's employers in June 2013 and Esme moved in on 1 August 2020.

The house had therefore been owned by the employer for more than six years when Esme first moved in.

Accordingly, the expensive accommodation benefit must be calculated using the market value of the house when Esme first moved in rather than the original cost.

22   LOACH

(a)   The answer is £Nil.

Tutorial note

Interest free and low interest loans which do not exceed £10,000 at any time in the tax year are an exempt benefit.

(b)   The answer is A.

Working

Expensive accommodation benefit

= ((£100,000 + £30,000) – £75,000) × 2.25% = £1,238

Tutorial note

The house was purchased by Margarita's employers in December 2014 and Margarita moved in on 1 November 2019.

The house had therefore been owned by the employer for less than six years when Margarita first moved in.

Accordingly, the expensive accommodation benefit must be calculated using the original cost of the house plus improvements up to the start of the tax year, and not the market value when Margarita first moved in.

The house has been available for the whole of the tax year 2020/21, therefore there is no need to time apportion the benefit.

(c)   Job related accommodation

	Job related	Not job related
Accommodation provided for a priest	✓	
Accommodation provided for a warden at a care home	✓	
Accommodation provided for directors to enable them to get to work more easily		✓

Tutorial note

*Accommodation provided for a priest and a care home warden is job related as it is provided for the **better performance of their duties** and it is **customary** for such employments to be provided with accommodation.*

Accommodation supplied for directors can only be job related if special security considerations apply.

(d)   The answer is £4,800.

Working

	£
Higher of: Annual value = £6,000, or	6,000
Rent paid by employer = (£450 × 12) = £5,400	
Less: Rent paid by Eve (£100 × 12)	(1,200)
Taxable benefit – 2020/21	4,800

(e)   True or false

	True	False
Furniture provided by an employer is taxed at 25% of the market value per annum		✓
Provision of workplace child care is an exempt benefit	✓	
A loan of £12,000 provided to an employee in order that they can buy items wholly, exclusively and necessarily for their employment are exempt from income tax	✓	
Reimbursement of expenses for home to work travel is not a taxable benefit for the employee.		✓
Provision of eye tests and spectacles for VDU use is an exempt benefit for an employee	✓	

Tutorial note

Furniture provided by an employer is taxed on the employee at 20% per annum of the market value when first made available to the employee.

*Loans which do not exceed £10,000 at any time in the tax year **or** which are made to allow employees to purchase items wholly exclusively and necessarily for employment are an exempt benefit.*

The expense relating to travel from home to work represents ordinary commuting and is not tax allowable.

23   BHARAT

(a)   The answer is £360.

   Working

   Use of asset benefit = (£3,600 × 20% × 6/12) = £360

Tutorial note

The benefit for the use of a company asset such as a home cinema system is 20% of the market value of the asset when first made available to the employee.

Bharat has only had use of the system for six months in the tax year 2020/21, therefore the benefit must be time apportioned.

(b)   The answer is **6** years.

(c)   Job related accommodation

	Job related	Not job related
Accommodation provided for a matron at a boarding school	✓	
Accommodation provided for the Prime Minister	✓	
Accommodation provided for a sales director so that he may entertain prospective customers. There are no special security considerations.		✓

Tutorial note

*Accommodation provided for a matron at a boarding school is job related as it is provided for the **better performance of the matron's duties** and it is **customary** for matron to be provided with accommodation.*

*Accommodation provided for the Prime Minister is **part of special arrangements to counter a special security threat** which arises from the job of being Prime Minister.*

Accommodation supplied for directors can only be job related if special security considerations apply.

(d)   The answer is £4,640.

   Working

		£
Higher of: Annual value = £5,600, or		5,600
Rent paid by employer = (£420 × 12) = £5,040		
Less: Rent paid by Sybil (£80 × 12)		(960)
Taxable benefit – 2020/21		4,640

(e)   The answer is C.

Tutorial note

Statements (iii) and (iv) are correct.

Furniture is a taxable benefit that is calculated as 20% of the market value of the furniture when first made available to the employee.

Therefore, statements (i) and (ii) are incorrect.

24   NIKITA

(a)   The answer is £175.

   Working

   Beneficial loan benefit = £28,000 × (2.25% – 1.0%) × 6/12 = £175

Tutorial note

Beneficial loan interest benefit is calculated as follows:

= Outstanding loan × the difference between the official rate of interest (2.25% in 2020/21) and the actual interest rate paid by the employee.

However, as the loan was provided for only six months of the tax year 2020/21, the benefit must be time apportioned as the rates of interest quoted are annual rates.

(b)   The answer is £3,490.

A standard figure of £3,490 applies for the van benefit in 2020/21.

(c)   The answer is £13,038.

Working

	£
Annual value	5,000
Additional charge for 'expensive' accommodation:	
(£150,000 – £75,000) × 2.25%	1,688
Furniture (20% × £40,000)	8,000
Heating bills	750
	15,438
Less: Rent paid by Molly (£200 × 12)	(2,400)
Taxable benefit – 2020/21	13,038

(d)   The answer is D.

Tutorial note

Statements (i) and (iv) are correct.

25   GIBBS

(a)   The answer is £8,638.

Working

	£
Annual value	6,500
Additional charge for 'expensive' accommodation:	
(£250,000 – £75,000) × 2.25%	3,938
	10,438
Less: Rent paid by Gibbs (£150 × 12)	(1,800)
Taxable benefit – 2020/21	8,638

Tutorial note

The accommodation was purchased by Gibbs's employers in May 2017 and Gibbs moved in on 20 December 2017.

The accommodation had therefore been owned by the employer for less than six years when Gibbs first moved in.

> *Accordingly, the expensive accommodation benefit must be calculated using the original cost of the house plus improvements up to the start of the tax year, and not the market value when Gibbs first moved in.*
>
> *The improvements in June 2020 are not included in the calculations for the 2020/21 benefit as they were incurred during the tax year, rather than before the start of the tax year.*
>
> *The cost of the improvements will however be included in next year's benefit calculation.*

(b) The answer is £6,100.

Working

	£
Furniture benefit (£20,000 × 20%)	4,000
Household expenses (Note)	2,100
Taxable benefit – 2020/21	6,100

Tutorial note

The cost of extending the garage is not a taxable benefit as it is capital expenditure (i.e. an improvement to the property). It will be included in the cost of the property for the purpose of calculating any additional charge for expensive accommodation in 2020/21.

(c) The answer is £400.

Working

	£
Payment under staff suggestion scheme – exempt	—
Telephone expenses	400
Taxable benefit – 2020/21	400

Tutorial note

Payments made under a staff suggestion scheme of up to £5,000 are exempt benefits.

Telephone bills paid by the employer are taxable benefits valued at the cost to the employer.

(d)   The answer is £Nil.

Tutorial note

Provision of free or subsidised meals in a canteen is a tax free benefit provided there are canteen facilities for all staff.

26   PERDITA

(a)

	Exempt	Not exempt
One mobile telephone per employee	✓	
Use of a pool car	✓	
Use of a van for a fortnight's camping holiday. There is no other private use.		✓
Provision of a car parking space in a multi-storey car park near the place of work	✓	
Provision of bicycles for staff who have worked for the company for at least seven years		✓
A birthday present for an employee, which cost the employer £40.	✓	
Provision of an interest free loan of £9,000 made on 6 April 2020 and written off on 5 April 2021 – provision of loan – write off of loan	 ✓	 ✓

Tutorial note

The van benefit is taxable unless the private use by the employee is incidental. The use of the van for a fortnight would not be considered incidental private use.

The provision of bicycles or cycling safety equipment to enable employees to get to and from work are exempt benefits, but only provided they are available to staff generally. Therefore, only being available to staff who have worked for the company for at least seven years would make the benefit taxable, not exempt.

Birthday presents costing less than £50 are exempt under the trivial benefits rules.

Loans which total no more than £10,000 at any time in the tax year are exempt. However, loans of any amount which are written off are a taxable benefit.

(b)   The benefit is £315

       This is calculated as ½ x (£16,000 + £12,000) x 2.25% = £315

Tutorial note

Under this method the benefit is calculated using the average loan balance. This is calculated as:

½ x (opening loan balance + closing loan balance)

The benefit is calculated as the average loan balance x official rate of interest (2.25% in 2020/21).

Any interest paid by the employee would be deducted from the benefit.

27   JOEY

(a)   £Nil

(b)   £5,000

(c)   £2,792

Tutorial note

There is no taxable benefit on a pool car.

The taxable benefit for a zero emission van is 80% of the basic charge of £3,490.

28   HF LTD

(a)   The answer is A.

Tutorial note

Provision of sport and recreational facilities open to staff but not the general public is an exempt benefit.

Payment of an employee's gym subscription of £450 would be taxed on the employee.

(b)   £50

(c)   20

(d)   10

29   JADEJA PLC

	Exempt	Not exempt	Partly exempt
Free annual health screening which costs the employer £350 per head.	✓		
An annual staff party which costs £220 per head		✓	
Payments of £7 per night for personal expenses when employees have to stay away from home elsewhere in the UK		✓	
Removal expenses of £12,000 paid to an employee who had to relocate to a new town when she was promoted			✓
A smart phone issued to all staff of manager grade	✓		

Tutorial note

(i)   The cost of one annual health screening per year is an exempt benefit.

(ii)   Staff parties are only exempt if they cost no more than £150 per head.

(iii)   Personal expense payments up to £5 per night in the UK are exempt, but if the payments exceed this limit they are taxable.

(iv)   The first £8,000 of removal expenses is exempt.

(v)   Smart phones are exempt in the same way as mobile phones (i.e. one phone per employee)

30 DHONI LTD

	Exempt	Taxable
Payment of £800 fees for office employees attending computer skills courses	✓	
A training course entitled 'What you need to know about being self-employed' for an employee who is shortly to be made redundant, which cost Dhoni Ltd £500.	✓	
Long service awards of £500 cash for employees completing 20 years' service		✓(Note i)
Private medical insurance for employees who work only in the UK		✓(Note ii)
A payment of £500 to an employee in accordance with the rules of the staff suggestion scheme.	✓	
Free eye tests for all staff working with computers	✓	

Tutorial note

(i) *In order to be exempt, long service awards must be no more than £50 for each year of service provided service is at least 20 years. The award must not be in cash and the recipient must not have had an award within the previous 10 years. A cash award would be taxable.*

(ii) *Private medical insurance is a taxable benefit unless it is for employees who are working outside the UK.*

INCOME FROM PROPERTY

31 GIORGIS

	True	False
Giorgis has bought a house which he intends to let furnished. The initial cost of providing the furniture will be an allowable cost when calculating taxable property income.		✓
Income from property is always taxed on the cash basis unless the taxpayer elects to use the accruals basis.		✓
When calculating an individual's property income any costs of improving the property are not allowable.	✓	
Property losses from furnished lettings can be deducted from profits on unfurnished lettings.	✓	
Property losses can be offset against an individual's total income in the tax year		✓

Property expenses incurred when the property is empty cannot be deducted from property income, even if the property is available to let	✓

Tutorial note

The first statement is false because it is only the cost of replacing domestic items that is allowable and not the cost of the original items.

The second statement is false because the cash basis is only automatic for taxpayers with gross rents not exceeding £150,000 (though these taxpayers can elect to use accruals basis instead). For taxpayers with gross rents exceeding this figure the accruals basis applies.

The third statement is true because improvements to the property are capital expenditure and are therefore not allowable.

The fourth statement is true because net rental income is found by netting off all the rental profits and losses of the year, irrespective of whether the properties are furnished or unfurnished.

The fifth statement is false because property losses can only be set against future property income, not the total income in the current tax year.

The sixth statement is false as property expenses can always be deducted from property income as long as the property is available to let and the expenses are incurred wholly and exclusively for the purposes of the property business.

32 HOWARD

(a)   The answer is D.

Tutorial note

Legal fees in respect of the purchase of the property are part of the cost of acquiring the property and are not allowable when calculating property income.

The purchase of a new free-standing gas fire is capital expenditure and would not be allowable.

(b)   The correct answer is £4,750.

Mileage allowances for residential landlords **are** calculated using the approved mileage allowance payments.

Working

	£
10,000 miles at 45p per mile	4,500
1,000 miles at 25p per mile	250
	4,750

Tutorial note

The approved mileage rates are provided in the assessment and can be claimed for the purposes of managing the rental properties only. These amounts are claimed instead of the actual motor expenses which are not allowable expenses here.

33   GOOGOOSH

	One bedroom flat £	Four bedroom house £
Income:		
(£500 × 8) + (£525 × 4)	6,100	
(£480 × 5)		2,400
Expenses:		
Insurance		
(£100 × 8) + (£120 × 4)	(1,280)	
Repairs	(450)	
Gardening (£20 × 5)		(100)
New bed (Note) (£620 – £130)	(490)	
Rental profit	3,880	2,300

Tutorial note

In the absence of any election and where gross rents are less than £150,000, property income will be assessed on the cash basis. Therefore the rent on the flat is assessed based on the amounts received during the tax year (£500 for May to December and £525 for January to April).

The insurance costs are calculated based on the actual amounts paid (£800 from April to November and £480 from December to March).

The gardener has been paid for five months' work during this tax year, as he was paid at the end of each month.

A deduction is available for the cost of replacing the bed with a similar item. The allowable amount is reduced by any proceeds from the sale of the original bed.

The property allowance is not relevant in this question as both the rent received and the expenses exceed £1,000.

34 SUNITA

	Three bedroom house £	Two bedroom flat £
Income:		
(£1,000 × 5) + (£1,000 × 4)	9,000	
Less: Irrecoverable debt relief	(1,000)	
	8,000	
(£600 × 9)		5,400
Expenses:		
Commission (£8,000 × 5%)	(400)	
Letting agency fees		(950)
Insurance (£400 × 11/12)		(367)
New lounge furniture (£1,100 – £180)		(920)
New dining furniture		0
Rental profit	7,600	3,163

Tutorial note

The question states that Sheila has elected to be taxed on the accruals basis therefore the actual dates of receipt and payment are not relevant.

All of the rent accrued should be brought into the computation, however, there is relief for the August rent which is irrecoverable.

Note that in the assessment if there is a pro forma already set up with narrative, and there is no specific place to put irrecoverable debt relief, it is acceptable to just enter in the rental income section the net rents actually received (i.e. £8,000 in this case) rather than two entries of rents accrued (£9,000) and the £1,000 irrecoverable debt deduction.

*If there is part private use of a property by the owner, then expenses which cannot be directly attributed to the let period must be time apportioned to exclude the period of private use. Expenses relating wholly and exclusively to the period when the property is **available for letting** are allowable, the property does not have to be actually let at that time. In this case the flat was occupied privately for 1 month so it was available for letting for 11 months and so only 11/12 of the insurance can be allowed.*

A deduction is available for the cost of replacing the lounge furniture with a similar item. The allowable amount is reduced by any proceeds from the sale of the original furniture.

No deduction is available for the dining furniture as this is not a replacement item, but is the initial purchase of a capital item.

The property allowance is not relevant in this question as both the rent received and the expenses exceed £1,000.

35 WILL

	Two bedroom cottage £	One bedroom flat £	Three bedroom house £
Income:			
(£500 × 12)	6,000		
(£3,600 × 9/12)		2,700	
(£4,320 × 11/12)			3,960
Expenses:			
Gardening (£50 × 12)	(600)		
Cleaning (£70 × 11)	(770)		
Repairs	(400)		
Water rates		(500)	
Insurance – flat		(500)	
Insurance – house			(1,200)
Dining furniture (£600 – £100)	(500)		
Rental profit	3,730	1,700	2,760

Tutorial note

In the absence of any election and where gross rents are less than £150,000, property income will be assessed on the cash basis. Therefore, the rent on the three bedroom house is assessed based on the amounts received during the tax year, i.e. 11 months of rent.

The cleaner has only been paid for 11 months work during the tax year. The insurance on the house which was paid during the tax year is deductible, rather than the insurance payable in respect of the tax year.

A deduction is available for the cost of replacing a domestic item with a similar domestic item. However, the allowable amount is reduced by any proceeds from the sale of the original asset.

The property allowance is not relevant in this question as both the rent received and the expenses exceed £1,000.

36   EDWARD

	Four bedroom house £	Two bedroom bungalow £
Income:		
(£7,200 × 10/12)	6,000	
(£550 × 6)		3,300
Expenses		
Advertising	(100)	
Council tax (£700 × 11/12)	(642)	(1,100)
Repairs		(150)
New sofa (£900 – £220)		(680)
Rental profit	5,258	1,370

Tutorial note

In the absence of any election and where gross rents are less than £150,000, property income will be assessed on the cash basis. Therefore the rent on the four bedroom house is assessed based on the amounts received during the tax year (allowing relief for the unpaid rent for February and taxing the rent paid on 1 April 2021).

Only 11/12 of the council tax expense on the four bedroom house is allowable as Edward was in the property for the month of March.

A deduction is available for the cost of replacing the sofa with a similar item. The allowable amount is reduced by any proceeds from the sale of the original sofa.

The property allowance is not relevant in this question as both the rent received and the expenses exceed £1,000.

37   REBECCA

	15 Olden Way £	29 Harrow Crescent £	42 Long Close £
Income:			
(£600 × 12 months)	7,200		
(£500 × 6 months)		3,000	
(£750 × 5 months)			3,750
Expenses:			
Insurance			
(£150 × 9/12 + £180 × 3/12)	(158)		
(£120 × 9/12 + £140 × 3/12)		(125)	
(£160 × 8/12)			(107)
Water rates	(80)	(100)	(85)
Furniture (£1,500 – £40)	(1,460)		(–)
	———	———	———
Rental profit	5,502	2,775	3,558
	———	———	———

Tutorial note

The question states that Rebecca has elected to be taxed on the accruals basis therefore the actual dates of receipt and payment are not relevant.

*Expenses are allowable on an accruals basis; therefore the insurance **accrued** in the tax year should be brought into the computation. It is therefore necessary to time apportion the expense.*

A deduction is available for the cost of replacing the bedroom furniture with similar items. The allowable amount is reduced by any proceeds from the sale of the original furniture.

No deduction is available in respect of the cost of the furniture for 42 Long Close because it did not replace existing furniture.

The property allowance is not relevant in this question as both the rent received and the expenses exceed £1,000.

38   ROSALIE

(a)   The answer is £2,070.

   Working

   Insurance expense = (£1,800 × 3/12) + (£2,160 × 9/12) = £2,070

Tutorial note

*Rosalie is assessed on the accruals basis as **her gross rents exceed £150,000.***

(b)   The answer is B.

(c)   The statement is true.

Tutorial note

Losses made on renting out a property can only be offset against property profits. If a taxpayer has more than one rental property profits and losses on individual properties can be netted off. If the taxpayer makes an overall loss they show property income for the year of £nil then carry forward this loss against future property income only.

(d)   The statement is false.

Tutorial note

Property losses which cannot be offset in the year they are incurred are carried forward against future property income profits. This treatment is automatic. Brought forward losses are offset against future property income profits as soon as possible.

39   PROPERTY ALLOWANCE

	True	False
The property allowance is always automatically applied, although the taxpayer can elect not to claim it		✓
When a taxpayer has rental income of less than £1,000, they do not have to disclose the income to HMRC	✓	
A taxpayer with gross rental income of more than £1,000 and expenses of less than £1,000 should always claim the property allowance	✓	
The time limit for elections with respect to the property allowance for the tax year 2020/21 is 31 January 2023	✓	

> **Tutorial note**
>
> *The property allowance is only automatically applied when gross rental income is £1,000 or less.*
>
> *A taxpayer with property income over £1,000 they have a choice of being assessed on:*
>
> 1   *Gross rents less expenses; or*
>
> 2   *Gross rents less £1,000 (property allowance).*
>
> *In exam questions where gross rents exceed £1,000 you should deduct the property allowance instead of expenses if these are less than £1,000 (as this will give the lower amount of assessable income).*

INVESTMENT INCOME

40   SOPHIE

(a)   £1,028

	£
Taxable dividend income	4,700
£500 × 0% (dividend allowance in higher rate band)	0
£1,500 × 0% (dividend allowance in additional rate band)	0
£2,700 × 38.1%	1,028
Income tax liability	1,028

(b)   £1,200

	£
Taxable savings income	4,300
£500 × 0% (savings allowance for a higher rate taxpayer)	0
£1,600 × 20% (remainder of basic rate band)	320
£2,200 × 40% (higher rate band)	880
Income tax liability	1,200

41   RAVI

	£
Tax payable on savings income	290
Tax payable on dividend income	900
Total tax due on investment income	1,190

Tutorial note

Ravi's trading profits are taxable as non-savings income. They use his personal allowance so the taxable amount of these is £9,500 (£22,000 - £12,500).

The dividends received from an ISA are exempt.

Ravi's total taxable income is £25,950 (£9,500 + £250 + £2,200 + £14,000), meaning he is a basic rate taxpayer.

When taxing his savings income he will get a savings allowance of £1,000. The tax is therefore £1,450 (£250 + £2,200 - £1,000) at 20%, giving £290.

When taxing his dividend the first £2,000 will be covered by the dividend allowance. The tax on the balance is calculated at 7.5%, giving £900 (£12,000 x 7.5%)

42   CASTILAS

(a)   The answer is A.

(b)   £420

	£
Taxable dividend income	7,600
£2,000 × 0% (dividend allowance)	0
£5,600 × 7.5% (basic rate)	420
Income tax liability	420

Tutorial note

The first £2,000 of taxable dividend income is always covered by the dividend allowance. As Ramos' total taxable income does not exceed £37,500 he is a basic rate taxpayer meaning the rest of the tax is calculated at 7.5%

(c)   £3,360

	£
Taxable savings income	8,900
£500 × 0% (savings allowance for a higher rate taxpayer)	0
£8,400 × 40% (higher rate)	3,360
Income tax on savings income	3,360

43   MARLON

(a)   £0

	£
Taxable dividend income (£3,300 – £1,500)	1,800
£1,800 × 0% (dividend allowance)	0
Income tax liability	0

(b)   £3,120

	£
Taxable savings income	8,300
£500 × 0% (savings allowance for a higher rate taxpayer)	0
£7,800 × 40% (higher rate band)	3,120
Income tax liability	3,120

44   KIRA

	Yes	No
Profit on disposal of an asset		✓
Rental profits	✓	
Tips earned whilst working in a bar	✓	
Damages for injury at work		✓

Tutorial note

The profit on the disposal of an asset is liable to capital gains tax, not income tax.

Compensation received for injury or death is tax free. It is important to learn the sources of exempt income for the exam.

Rental income is subject to income tax, as is employment income, including tips.

45   GINNY

Investment income

Exempt from income tax	Taxable
Interest from NS&I Savings Certificates Interest from Individual Savings Accounts (ISAs)	Interest from building society accounts Interest from bank accounts NS&I bank interest Interest from Gilts (Government stocks)

46   TARAN

    (a)   In 2020/21 the maximum amount that Taran (aged 42) can invest in an ISA is £...20,000............

    (b)   The statement is true.

    (c)   The statement is true.

Tutorial note

The maximum that an individual aged 18 or over can invest in an ISA in 2020/21 is £20,000. This figure covers total investments in all ISA products for the year.

Note that those aged 16 and over can invest in a cash only ISA, however only those aged 18 or over can invest in a stocks and shares ISA.

Income received from an ISA is exempt.

Gains realised on disposal of stocks and shares in an ISA are exempt from capital gains tax.

---

47   HUANG

    (a)   £1,560

	£
Taxable savings income	3,700
£0 × 0% (savings allowance for an additional rate taxpayer)	0
£2,100 × 40% (remainder of higher rate band)	840
£1,600 × 45% (higher rate band)	720
Income tax liability	1,560

    (b)   £195

	£
Taxable dividend income	2,600
£2,000 × 0% (dividend allowance for a higher rate taxpayer)	0
£600 × 32.5%	195
Income tax liability	195

COMPUTATION OF TAXABLE INCOME AND OTHER MATTERS

48   JESSICA

    (a)   The tax year runs from 6 April 2020 to 5 April 2021 and Jessica's salary changes after one month of this period. Jessica received an annual salary of £36,300 for one month and £20,000 for 11 months.

        Taxable salary for 2020/21 = (£36,300 × 1/12) + (£20,000 × 11/12) = £21,358.

(b) The taxable bonus for 2020/21 is £2,300.

This is the bonus received in 2020/21.

The accounting year to which it relates is not relevant.

(c) The commission received in 2020/21 is £1,602 (£21,358 × 7.5%).

49 JANE

(a) The answer is £19,500

The tax year runs from 6 April 2020 to 5 April 2021 and Jane's salary changes after three months of this period. Jane received an annual salary of £18,000 for three months and £20,000 for nine months.

Taxable salary for 2020/21 = (£18,000 × 3/12) + (£20,000 × 9/12) = £19,500

(b) The answer is £1,000.

The taxable bonus in 2020/21 is the one received during 2020/21.

(c) The taxable commission in 2020/21 is the amount received in the year of £1,170 (£19,500 × 6%).

50 EFFIE

The answer is £31,320.

	£
Salary (£30,000 × 6/12 + £33,600 × 6/12)	31,800
Reimbursed expenses (see note)	0
Less: Payroll giving contribution	(480)
Taxable employment income	31,320

Tutorial note

The tax year runs from 6 April 2020 to 5 April 2021 and Effie's salary changes after six months of this period. Effie received an annual salary of £30,000 for six months and £33,600 for six months.

The contribution to charity under the payroll giving scheme is an allowable deduction from employment income.

However, a gift aid donation is not deducted from employment income. Relief is available for the donation, but not as an allowable deduction from employment income.

Instead, basic rate relief is given at source as payments to the charity are paid net of 20% tax. Higher rate and additional rate relief is given by extending the basic rate band and higher rate band by the gross gift aid donation.

Reimbursed employment expenses are included as part of employment income unless, as in this situation, a tax deduction would be available to the employee in respect of the costs incurred.

51 HUI

(a) Hui's taxable salary for 2020/21 is £16,500 (£1,300 × 9) + (£1,600 × 3).

Tutorial note

The tax year runs from 6 April 2020 to 5 April 2021 and Hui's salary changes after nine months of this period. Hui received a monthly salary of £1,300 for nine months and £1,600 for three months.

(b) Hui's taxable bonus for 2020/21 is **£1,125 paid** to him during the tax year on 15 April 2020.

52 MANINDER

The answer is £27,110.

	£
Salary	25,000
Round sum expense allowance (amount spent on entertaining) (30%)	3,600
	28,600
Less: Allowable deductions	
Pension contribution (£25,000 × 5%)	(1,250)
Payroll giving (£20 × 12)	(240)
Taxable employment income	27,110

Tutorial note

Any part of a round sum allowance which is spent on entertaining is included as taxable employment income.

53 SALLY

(a) The answer is C.

	£
Received (20,000 × 25p)	5,000
Less: Allowable under HMRC rules:	
10,000 × 45p	(4,500)
10,000 × 25p	(2,500)
Allowable employment income expense	(2,000)

(b)   The answer is A.

Tutorial note

Contributions to an occupational pension scheme are paid gross and deducted from earnings for tax purposes.

Pension contributions made by an employer are an exempt benefit.

(c)   The answer is C.

Tutorial note

When an employee receives a round sum allowance for expenses, they are taxed on the allowance received less what they spend on business expenses EXCEPT entertaining customers/potential customers.

(d)   The answer is C.

Tutorial note

The question asks which statement is ALWAYS true.

The options A and B may or may not be true. Option D is not true.

54   BERNIE

	True	False
Bernie cannot contribute to both a personal pension scheme and to his employer's occupational scheme.		✓
Personal pension scheme payments are made net of 10% tax.		✓
Relief for occupational pension payments is given by deducting the payments made from gross earnings.	✓	
Gary pays a cheque for £260 to his personal pension scheme. He will obtain tax relief by extending his basic rate band by £260.		✓
Sobia is currently unemployed and has no earnings. She cannot contribute to a personal pension scheme because she has no relevant earnings.		✓
Pension contributions made by an employer on behalf of an employee are a taxable benefit.		✓

Tutorial note

An individual can contribute to both personal and occupational pension schemes.

Gary will pay his personal pension contribution net of 20% tax. The grossed up amount of £325 (£260 × 100/80) increases the threshold for higher rate and additional rate tax purposes.

Sobia can contribute up to £3,600 (gross amount) to her personal pension scheme even if she has no earnings.

Contributions made by an employer are an exempt benefit.

55 **RON**

(a) The answer is C.

	£
Received (18,000 × 38p)	6,840
Less: Allowable under HMRC rules:	
10,000 × 45p	(4,500)
8,000 × 25p	(2,000)
Taxable employment income	340

(b) The answer is D.

Tutorial note

Political donations are not tax allowable.

(c) The answer is B.

Tutorial note

Occupational pension scheme contributions are paid gross and deducted from employment income.

Employer contributions to pension schemes are not a taxable benefit.

(d) (i) £3,600

(ii) 100%

56   ASIF

(a)   The answer is C.

Tutorial note

Payroll giving donations are tax deductible. Gift aid donations are not allowable deductions from employment income.

Relief for gift aid donations is available by giving basic rate relief at source and by extending the basic rate and higher rate bands.

(b)   The answer is D.

Tutorial note

Statement (ii) is incorrect because personal pension contributions are not deducted from income. Instead, relief is available by giving basic rate relief at source and by extending the basic rate and higher rate bands.

*Statement (v) is incorrect because the maximum pension contribution is the **higher** of £3,600 and 100% of relevant earnings.*

(c)   The answer is B.

	£
Received (20,000 × 28p)	5,600
Less: Allowable under HMRC rules:	
10,000 × 45p	(4,500)
4,000 × 25p	(1,000)
Taxable employment income	100

Tutorial note

Home to work travel is not business travel and therefore not allowable under the HMRC rules. If the employer pays more than the HMRC approved amounts the excess is added to employment income. If they pay less the difference can be deducted.

57 ARKAN

	£
Salary	91,350
Personal pension scheme	0
Bonus	5,000
Car benefit	5,500
Dividend	11,000
Building society interest	750
Interest from ISA	0
Personal allowance	8,555
Taxable income	105,045

Workings

(W1) Taxable income

	£
Salary (£90,000 × 6/12) + (£90,000 × 1.03 × 6/12)	91,350
Personal pension scheme (not an allowable deduction)	0
Bonus (received in tax year)	5,000
Car benefit	5,500
Dividend	11,000
Building society interest	750
Interest from ISA (exempt)	0
Net income	113,600
Personal allowance (W2)	(8,555)
Taxable income	105,045

(W2) Personal allowance

	£	£
Personal allowance		12,500
Net income	113,600	
Less: Gross personal pension contribution		
(£91,350 × 5% × 100/80)	(5,709)	
Adjusted net income	107,891	
Less: Limit	(100,000)	
Excess	7,891 × 50%	(3,945)
Adjusted PA		8,555

58 PHLOX

	£
Pension	15,075
Dividend from Enterprise plc	5,000
ISA dividend	0
Building society interest	7,500
NS&I bank interest	705
Gift aid payment	0
Gain on shares	0
Personal allowance	12,500
Taxable income	15,780

Workings

(W1) Taxable income

	£
Pension (£15,000 × 9/12) + (£15,000 × 1.02 × 3/12)	15,075
Dividend from Enterprise)	5,000
ISA dividend (exempt)	0
Building society interest	7,500
NS&I bank interest	705
Gift aid payment (not an allowable deduction)	0
Gain on shares (capital not income)	0
Net income	28,280
Personal allowance	(12,500)
Taxable income	15,780

59 ALEXIS

	£
Salary	41,167
Commission	1,200
Contribution to employer pension scheme	2,058
Employer's pension contribution	0
Mileage allowance – taxable amount	0
Mileage allowance – tax allowable expense	600
Dividend	1,000
Building society interest	437
Interest from ISA	0
Personal allowance	12,500
Taxable income	28,646

Workings

(W1) Taxable income

	£
Salary (£40,000 × 5/12) + (£42,000 × 7/12)	41,167
Commission (1% × £120,000) paid 1 May 2020	1,200
Contribution to employer pension scheme (£41,167 × 5%)	(2,058)
Employer's pension contribution (exempt benefit)	0
Mileage allowance (W2) – expense	(600)
Dividend	1,000
Building society interest	437
Interest from ISA – exempt	0
Net income	41,146
Personal allowance	(12,500)
Taxable income	28,646

(W2) Mileage allowance

	£
Mileage allowance received (14,000 × 35p)	4,900
Less: Allowable under HMRC rules	
10,000 × 45p	(4,500)
4,000 × 25p	(1,000)
Allowable expense	(600)

60   DOMINIC

Dominic will pay £3,780 (£54,000 × 7%) into the scheme. This will be grossed up at 100/80 to give a gross contribution of £4,725. This amount can affect the tax liability in two ways:

1   The grossed up amount reduces net income for the purposes of calculating restrictions on the personal allowance for taxpayers with income over £100,000. This does not affect Dominic in 2020/21.

2   The grossed up amount extends the basic rate band so that less income is taxed in the higher rate band and more in the basic rate band.

Dominic has taxable income of £41,500 (£54,000 – £12,500). Before making the pension contribution, £4,000 (£41,500 – £37,500) of this income is taxed at the higher rate. The effect of the contribution of £4,725 is that all of his income will now be taxed at the basic rate of 20% rather than the higher rate of 40% saving him £800 (£4,000 × (40% – 20%)).

The net after tax cost to Dominic of making the payment is £2,980 (£3,780 – £800).

61   EMPLOYMENT STATUS

	Employment	Self-employment
Contract for services is for		✓
Contract of service is for	✓	
A worker providing their own tools to perform the work would indicate		✓

Tutorial note

A self-employed individual is contracted to perform a task, to produce an end result. He is contracted for his services provided.

However, an employee has a contract of service and is required to perform all tasks asked of him by his employer whilst in the service of the business that employs him.

Provision of own equipment is one of the factors HMRC will consider to decide the status of the individual, and indicates that the relationship is more likely to be that of self-employment.

62   EMPLOYMENT OR SELF-EMPLOYMENT

	Employment	Self-employment
Minimal degree of control exercised		✓
Being personally responsible for poor work		✓
Provision of sick and holiday pay	✓	
Being able to hire helpers		✓
Carrying out an engagement for a long period	✓	
Regular payment on a monthly basis	✓	

Key answer tips

You need to make sure that you know the factors that HMRC will consider in order to decide the status of an individual with regard to employment or self-employment.

COMPUTATION OF TAX PAYABLE AND PAYMENT OF TAX

63   MARYAM

Income tax computation – 2020/21

		Total
		£
Property income	(£48,000 - £600)	47,400
Interest		250
ISA		0
Dividends		14,000
Net income		61,650
Less: PA		(12,500)
Taxable income		49,150

Income tax:		
Non-savings – basic rate	34,900 × 20%	6,980
Savings – savings allowance	250 × 0%	0
Dividends – dividend allowance	2,000 × 0%	0
Dividends – basic rate (W)	950 × 7.5%	71
Dividends – higher rate	11,050 × 32.5%	3,591
	49,150	
Income tax liability		10,642

Tutorial note

Maryam's property loss is automatically deducted from her property income. The net figure is assessable as non-savings income.

The personal allowance is deducted from non-savings income in priority to her savings and dividend income. The taxable non-savings income is £34,900 (£47,400 - £12,500).

Working: Extended basic rate band

	£
Basic rate band	37,500
Plus: Gift aid (£40 × 100/80 x 12)	600
Extended basic rate band	38,100

Tutorial note

Maryam's basic rate band can be extended by the gross amount of her gift aid donations.

Although her income falling within the savings and dividend allowances is taxable at 0%, this income uses up the basic rate band in priority to other dividend income.

The basic rate band remaining for the dividends is calculated as:

£38,100 - £34,900 - £250 - £2,000 = £950

Key answer tips

In the exam you could be provided with a grid consisting of either three or five columns so you must be prepared to deal with either situation.

If faced with three columns a useful approach is to write up the full five column approach on paper then type up the total column into the grid in your exam.

Remember you will not be able to include totals lines in your answer but do not worry about this, the marker will be able to follow when you are adding down as long as your answer is clearly labelled.

64   LUCIA

Income tax computation – 2020/21

	Non-savings	Savings	Dividends	Total
	£	£	£	£
Employment income	40,000			40,000
Lottery winnings	0			0
Savings income		800		800
Dividends			18,000	18,000
Net income	40,000	800	18,000	58,800
Less: PA	(12,500)			(12,500)
Taxable income	27,500	800	18,000	46,300

Income tax:		
Non-savings – basic rate	27,500 × 20%	5,500
Savings – savings allowance	500 × 0%	0
Savings – basic rate	300 × 20%	60
Dividends – dividend allowance	2,000 × 0%	0
Dividends – basic rate	8,200 × 7.5%	615
Dividends – higher rate	7,800 × 32.5%	2,535
	46,300	
Income tax liability		8,710

Tutorial note

Lucia is a higher rate taxpayer as her total taxable income exceeds £37,500. This means she is entitled to a savings allowance of £500.

Working: Extended basic rate band

	£
Basic rate band	37,500
Plus: Gift aid (2% × £40,000 × 100/80)	1,000
Extended basic rate band	38,500

Tutorial note

Sofia's basic rate band can be extended by the gross amount of her personal pension contributions.

Key answer tips

It is important when using this type of layout to analyse the taxable income into 'non-savings income', 'savings' and 'dividends' as different rates of tax apply to the different sources of income.

Note that:

- The above layout should be possible if the CBA gives at least four columns to complete the calculation.

- The total lines do not have to be inserted in the real CBA.

- You may find it useful to do the computation on paper first before inputting on screen.

- If the source of income is not specified in the CBA, always assume it is 'non-savings income'.

- It is acceptable to have the total column on the right rather than on the left if you prefer. However, we recommend that the analysis columns are in the fixed order: 'non-savings income', 'savings' and then 'dividends', as this is the order in which they must be taxed through the bands. Nil columns are not required.

65 ROMAN

Income tax computation – 2020/21

	Non-savings £	Savings £	Dividends £	Total £
Pension	23,626			23,626
Property income	3,000			3,000
Savings income		2,720		2,720
Dividends			6,144	6,144
Net income	26,626	2,720	6,144	35,490
Less: PA	(12,500)			(12,500)
Taxable income	14,126	2,720	6,144	22,990

Income tax:		
Non-savings – basic rate	14,126 × 20%	2,825
Savings – savings allowance	1,000 × 0%	0
Savings – basic rate	1,720 × 20%	344
Dividends – dividend allowance	2,000 × 0%	0
Dividends – basic rate	4,144 × 7.5%	311
	22,990	
Income tax liability		3,480

Tutorial note

Roman's pension income is taxable income and is treated as earned 'non-savings income'.

As Roman is a basic rate taxpayer he is entitled to a savings allowance of £1,000. All taxpayers are entitled to a dividend allowance of £2,000.

66   RAY

Income tax computation – 2020/21

	Non-savings £	Savings £	Total £
Income	50,870		50,870
Savings income		3,700	3,700
Net income	50,870	3,700	54,570
Less: PA	(12,500)		(12,500)
Taxable income	38,370	3,700	42,070

Income tax:		
Non-savings – basic rate	38,000 (W) × 20%	7,600
Non-savings – higher rate	370 × 40%	148
Savings – savings allowance	500 × 0%	0
Savings – higher rate	3,200 × 40%	1,280
	42,070	
Income tax liability		9,028

Tutorial note

As Ray is a higher rate taxpayer he is entitled to a savings allowance of £500.

Working: Extended basic rate band

	£
Basic rate band	37,500
Plus: Gift aid (£400 × 100/80)	500
Extended basic rate band	38,000

Key answer tips

It is important when using this type of layout to analyse the taxable income into 'non-savings income', 'savings' and 'dividends' as different rates of tax apply to the different sources of income.

Note that:

- The above layout should be possible if the CBA gives at least four columns to complete the calculation.

- The total lines do not have to be inserted in the real CBA.

- You may find it useful to do the computation on paper first before inputting on screen. This will be especially useful if you are only given three columns to complete in the assessment – where you will only include the total column on screen.

- If the source of income is not specified in the CBA, always assume it is 'non-savings income'.

- It is acceptable to have the total column on the right rather than on the left if you prefer. However, we recommend that the analysis columns are in the fixed order: 'non-savings income', 'savings' and then 'dividends', as this is the order in which they must be taxed through the bands.

67   JJ

Income tax computation – 2020/21

	Non-savings	Savings	Dividends	Total
	£	£	£	£
Employment income	148,200			148,200
BSI		7,150		7,150
Dividends			7,556	7,556
Net income	148,200	7,150	7,556	162,906
Less: PA (Note)	(0)			(0)
Taxable income	148,200	7,150	7,556	162,906

Income tax:		
Non-savings – basic rate	37,500 × 20%	7,500
Non-savings – higher rate	110,700 × 40%	44,280
Savings – higher rate	1,800 × 40%	720
	150,000	
Savings – additional rate	5,350 × 45%	2,407
Dividends – dividend allowance	2,000 × 0%	0
Dividends – additional rate	5,556 × 38.1%	2,117
	162,906	
Income tax liability		57,024

Tutorial note

The personal allowance is reduced to £Nil as JJ has adjusted net income > £125,000.

Adjusted net income = net income less gross gift aid donations and gross personal pension contributions. As JJ has not made such payments, his net income = his adjusted net income.

As JJ is an additional rate taxpayer he is not entitled to a savings allowance. All taxpayers are entitled to a dividend allowance of £2,000.

Key answer tips

It is important when using this type of layout to analyse the taxable income into 'non-savings income', 'savings' and 'dividends' as different rates of tax apply to the different sources of income.

Note that:

- The above layout should be possible if the CBA gives five columns to complete the calculation.
- The total lines do not have to be inserted in the real CBA.
- You may find it useful to do the computation on paper first before inputting on screen. This will be especially useful if you are only given three columns to complete in the assessment – where you will only include the total column on screen.
- If the source of income is not specified in the CBA, always assume it is 'non-savings income'.
- It is acceptable to have the total column on the right rather than on the left if you prefer. However, we recommend that the analysis columns are in the fixed order: 'non-savings income', 'savings' and then 'dividends', as this is the order in which they must be taxed through the bands.

68   BILL

Income tax computation – 2020/21

	Non-savings £	Savings £	Total £
Employment income	54,600		54,600
BSI		3,000	3,000
Net income	54,600	3,000	57,600
Less: PA	(12,500)		(12,500)
Taxable income	42,100	3,000	45,100
Income tax:			
Non-savings – basic rate	37,500 × 20%		7,500
Non-savings – higher rate	4,600 × 40%		1,840
Savings – savings allowance	500 × 0%		0
Savings – higher rate	2,500 × 40%		1,000
	45,100		
Income tax liability			10,340
Less: Tax credits			
PAYE			(9,340)
Income tax payable			1,000

Tutorial note

As Bill is a higher rate taxpayer he is entitled to a savings allowance of £500.

Key answer tips

It is important when using this type of layout to analyse the taxable income into 'non-savings income', 'savings' and 'dividends' as different rates of tax apply to the different sources of income.

Note that:

- The above layout should be possible provided the CBA gives four columns to complete the calculation.
- The total lines do not have to be inserted in the real CBA.
- You may find it useful to do the computation on paper first before inputting on screen. This will be especially useful if you are only given three columns to complete in the assessment – where you will only include the total column on screen.
- If the source of income is not specified in the CBA, always assume it is 'non-savings income'.
- It is acceptable to have the total column on the right rather than on the left if you prefer. However, we recommend that the analysis columns are in the fixed order: 'non-savings income', 'savings' and then 'dividends', as this is the order in which they must be taxed through the bands.

If you are only provided with 3 columns then this layout will be appropriate

Workings		£
Employment income		54,600
BSI		3,000
Net income		57,600
Less: PA		(12,500)
Taxable income		45,100
Income tax:		
Non-savings – basic rate	37,500 × 20%	7,500
Non-savings – higher rate (£54,600 – £12,500 – £37,500)	4,600 × 40%	1,840
Savings – savings allowance	500 × 0%	0
Savings – higher rate	2,500 × 40%	1,000
	45,100	
Income tax liability		10,340
Less: Tax credits – PAYE		(9,340)
Income tax payable		1,000

69 FENFANG

Income tax computation – 2020/21

	Non-savings	Dividends	Total
	£	£	£
Employment income	70,000		70,000
Dividends		40,200	40,200
Net income	70,000	40,200	110,200
Less: Adjusted PA (W1)	(8,750)		(8,750)
Taxable income	61,250	40,200	101,450
Income tax:			
Non-savings – basic rate	40,200 × 20% (W2)		8,040
Non-savings – higher rate	21,050 × 40%		8,420
	61,250		
Dividends – dividend allowance	2,000 × 0%		0
Dividends – higher rate	38,200 × 32.5%		12,415
	101,450		
Income tax liability			28,875
Less: Tax credit			
PAYE			(15,500)
Income tax payable			13,375

Workings

(W1) Adjusted personal allowance

	£	£
Personal allowance		12,500
Net income	110,200	
Less: PPC (£2,000 × 100/80)	(2,500)	
Gift aid (£160 × 100/80)	(200)	
Adjusted net income	107,500	
Less: Limit	(100,000)	
Excess	7,500 × 50%	(3,750)
Adjusted PA		8,750

(W2) Extended basic and higher rate bands

	BR band	HR band
	£	£
Basic rate/Higher rate bands	37,500	150,000
Plus: PPC (£2,000 × 100/80)	2,500	2,500
Gift aid (£160 × 100/80)	200	200
Extended bands	40,200	152,700

Tutorial note

As Fenfang's adjusted net income exceeds £100,000, her personal allowance must be reduced.

Adjusted net income = net income less gross gift aid donations and gross personal pension contributions.

As Fenfang has made both a personal pension payment and gift aid donation, her 'adjusted net income' needs to be calculated and compared to the £100,000 limit.

In addition, her basic rate and higher rate bands need to be extended by the gross personal pension contribution and gift aid donation to determine the appropriate rate of tax to apply.

As her income falls below the extended £152,700 additional rate threshold, her income in excess of £40,200 is taxed at 40% (non-savings income) and 32.5% (dividends).

All taxpayers are entitled to a dividend allowance of £2,000.

Key answer tips

It is important when using this type of layout to analyse the taxable income into 'non-savings income', 'savings' and 'dividends' as different rates of tax apply to the different sources of income.

Note that:

- The above layout should be possible provided the CBA gives four columns to complete the calculation.

- The total lines do not have to be inserted in the real CBA.

- You may find it useful to do the computation on paper first before inputting on screen. This will be especially useful if you are only given three columns to complete in the assessment – where you will only include the total column on screen.

- If the source of income is not specified in the CBA, always assume it is 'non-savings income'.

- It is acceptable to have the total column on the right rather than on the left if you prefer. However, we recommend that the analysis columns are in the fixed order: 'non-savings income', 'savings' and then 'dividends', as this is the order in which they must be taxed through the bands.

TAX MINIMISATION

70   ARON AND VIKTOR

(a)   C.

Tutorial note

All taxpayers are entitled to a dividend allowance of £2,000. Aron should retain sufficient shares to generate dividends of £2,000 himself thus using this.

The remaining shares should be transferred to Viktor. This will also use his dividend allowance. As Viktor is a basic rate taxpayer it is more tax efficient for the remaining dividends to be taxed on him at 7.5% rather than on Aron at 38.1% (as he is an additional rate taxpayer.

(b)　Mark the following statements as true or false

	True	False
Paloma's only income is employment income of £45,000. Paloma can receive savings income of up to a maximum of £500 without having any further income tax liability.		✓
All taxpayers, regardless of the rate of tax they pay, can receive tax-free dividend income of £2,000 per year.	✓	
Nita has net income of £106,000 a year. To receive a full personal allowance in 2020/21 she must make gift aid donations of £4,800	✓	

Tutorial note

The first statement is false as Paloma has £5,200 of her basic rate band remaining (£37,500 – (£45,000 – £12,500)). She therefore has a savings allowance of £1,000 and can received up to £1,000 of savings income without becoming a higher rate taxpayer and therefore, without having any further income tax liability.

The second statement is true. The dividend allowance is available to all taxpayers.

The third statement is true. This will give Nita adjusted net income of £100,000 (£106,000 – 100/80 £4,800) meaning the full personal allowance is available.

71　CRISPIN AND AMANA

(a)　Crispin and Amana

Bank interest income

Crispin is an additional rate taxpayer and therefore is not entitled to a savings allowance.

Amana is currently a basic rate taxpayer who is not utilising her savings allowance.

It would be more tax efficient if all of Crispin's bank interest were realised by Amana. £1,000 would be covered by her savings allowance as she is a basic rate taxpayer. The remainder would be taxed at 20% (basic rate for savings income) rather than 45% for Crispin.

Dividend income

Crispin is using the whole of his dividend allowance. The excess of his dividend income over the allowance is taxed at 38.1% because he is an additional rate taxpayer.

Amana is not using any of her dividend allowance.

It would be more tax efficient if £9,500 of Crispin's dividend income were realised by Amana. She would then use the whole of her dividend allowance. The excess of her dividend income over the dividend allowance of £7,500 (£9,500 – £2,000) would be taxed at 7.5% in her hands rather than at 38.1% in the hands of Crispin.

The remainder of Crispin's dividend income of £2,000 would be covered by his dividend allowance and taxed at 0%.

Tutorial note

In the sample assessment task 8(b) also tests tax planning between a husband and wife. However, it is not a written task and does not give as much detail as the task shown here about the types of investment income received. The only answer options available are to give all the investment income to either spouse, or to split it equally between them. In this situation, the correct answer is to give all the income to the spouse paying basic rate tax, since a more sophisticated tax planning solution such as that shown above is not an option.

(b)   Mark the following statements as true or false

	True	**False**
Flora is provided with a £9,000 loan by her employer. She has never been lent money by her employer before. In order for this loan to be tax free, the employer must charge interest above 2.5%.		✓
Dexter's only income is rent received of £12,000. His expenses in relation to this letting are £780. Dexter can receive dividend income of up to a maximum of £3,500 without having any income tax liability.	✓	

Tutorial note

The first statement is false. As Flora only has one loan of less than £10,000 from her employer it will be an exempt benefit even if no interest is charged.

Dexter has property income of £11,000 (£12,000 – £1,000). This is because he can elect to deduct the property allowance of £1,000 from his rental income, rather than his expenses, which are lower. His property income is all covered by the personal allowance and there is £1,500 of personal allowance remaining (£12,500 - £11,000). This can be set against his dividend income and a further £2,000 of his dividend income is taxed at 0% due to the dividend allowance.

72 FREYA

(i) Contribution of £2,000 towards the capital cost of the car

The CO_2 emissions of 113 g/km are rounded down to 110 g/km. The appropriate percentage is therefore 25% (14% + (110 – 55) × 1/5).

Freya's capital contribution will reduce the list price by £2,000. Her taxable benefit will therefore be reduced by £500 (2,000 × 25%).

Freya is a higher rate taxpayer. Her tax liability will therefore fall by £200 (£500 × 40%) per year.

(ii) Contribution of £600 per year towards the cost of using the car for private purposes

This contribution will reduce the taxable benefit by £600.

Freya's tax liability will therefore fall by £240 (£600 × 40%).

(iii) Contribution of £480 per year towards the cost of the private use petrol

This will not have any effect on Freya's income tax liability because she will not be paying the whole of the cost of the petrol used for private purposes. Unless she pays for all her private fuel she is not entitled to a deduction for any partial contributions made and thus makes no saving on the £480 contribution.

73 MITCHELL

(i) Contribution of £5,700 towards the capital cost of the car

The CO_2 emissions of 116 g/km are rounded down to 115 g/km. The appropriate percentage is therefore 32% (14% + ((115 – 55) × 1/5) + 4% + 2%).

Mitchell's capital contribution will reduce the list price by £5,000 (the maximum amount). His taxable benefit will therefore be reduced by £1,600 (5,000 × 32%).

Mitchell is a basic rate taxpayer. His tax liability will therefore fall by £320 (£1,600 × 20%) per year.

(ii) The cost of accessories added to the car after it was first provided will be added to the list price if they cost £100 or more.

Therefore the £185 of accessories will increase the benefit by £59 (£185 × 32%).

Mitchell's income tax liability will therefore be increased by £12 (£59 × 20%).

(iii) If the car had been registered on 6 April 2020, it would not suffer the additional 2%. The appropriate percentage would therefore be 30%

This will reduce the benefit by £446 (£22,300 × 2%).

Mitchell's tax liability will therefore fall by £89 (£446 × 20%).

NATIONAL INSURANCE CONTRIBUTIONS

74   TING

	True	False
Ting has attained state pension age but continues to work part-time earning £20,000 per year. Ting's employer has to pay national insurance contributions in respect of her earnings.	✓	
Bo is 47 years old. He is a self-employed entertainer at children's parties making a profit of £35,000 per year. Bo is required to pay class 1 employee contributions in respect of this profit.		✓
Michael is 32 years old. In 2020/21 he earned a gross salary of £37,000. He contributed £3,800 to an occupational pension scheme during the year. Michael's total liability to national insurance contributions for 2020/21 is £3,300.00 ((£37,000 – £9,500) x 12%).	✓	

Tutorial note

The first statement is true because employer's class 1 contributions are payable regardless of the age of the employee.

The second statement is false because Bo is self-employed and not an employee.

The third statement is true. Pension contributions are not deducted when calculating earnings for the purposes of national insurance contributions.

75   JEREMY

(a)   The answer is £31,000

Jeremy's earnings for the purposes of class 1 national insurance contributions consist of his salary only.

(b)   The answer is £993.60

Working

(£4,100 + £3,100) × 13.8%   £993.60
                                                                                    ‾‾‾‾‾‾‾‾‾‾

Tutorial note

The free parking space is an exempt benefit, such that it is not subject to class 1A contributions.

76   MURRAY

(a)   The answer is £6,380.00

Working

	£
(£50,000 – £9,500) × 12%	4,860.00
(£126,000 – £50,000) × 2%	1,520.00
	6,380.00

(b)   The answer is £16,175.26

Working

(£126,000 – £8,788) × 13.8%	£16,175.26

(c)   The answer is £1,987.20

Working

	£
Benefit in respect of company car and fuel	14,400
Free meals with all of the company's employees	0
	14,400
£14,400 × 13.8%	1,987.20

Tutorial note

No deduction is available for pension contributions or expenses incurred wholly, exclusively and necessarily in the performance of duties when calculating earnings for the purposes of national insurance contributions.

The free meals in the company's canteen are an exempt benefit, such that they are not subject to class 1A contributions.

77   LUKA

(a)   The answer is £5,012

Working	£
(£50,000 − £9,500) × 12%	4,860
(£57,600 (£4,800 × 12) − £50,000) × 2%	152
	5,012

(b)   The answer is £6,736

Working	
(£57,600 − £8,788) × 13.8%	£6,736

(c)   The answer is £1,145

Working	
£8,300 × 13.8%	£1,145

78   LEWIS

(a)   The answer is £5,500.00

Working	£
(£50,000 − £9,500) × 12%	4,860.00
(£71,000 + £11,000 − £50,000) × 2%	640.00
	5,500.00

(b)   The answer is £10,103.26

Working	
(£71,000 + £11,000 − £8,788) × 13.8%	£10,103.26

(c)   The answer is £757.62

Working	£
Benefit in respect of company car and fuel	5,100
Benefit in respect of camera on long term loan	390
	5,490
£5,490 × 13.8%	757.62

79   AMBER

	True	False
Amber is 56 years old. In 2020/21 she earned a salary of £40,000. She was also provided with a company car resulting in a taxable benefit of £3,700. Amber's total liability to national insurance contributions for 2020/21 is £4,104.00 ((£40,000 + £3,700 – £9,500) x 12%).		✓
John is 71 years old and receives a state pension. He is employed by Dory Ltd and was paid a gross salary of £118,000 in 2020/21. John does not have to pay any national insurance contributions in respect of his earnings from Dory Ltd	✓	
Philip is 77 years old and receives a state pension. He works part-time for Innes Ltd and earned £380 per month in 2020/21. Innes Ltd has to pay national insurance contributions in respect of Philip's earnings.		✓

Tutorial note

The first statement is false because employees do not pay class 1 contributions in respect of benefits.

The second statement is true because employees are not required to pay class 1 national insurance contributions once they have attained state pension age.

The third statement is false. Although employer's class 1 contributions are payable regardless of the age of the employee, Philip's annual earnings are only £4,560 (£380 × 12), which is less than £8,788.

80   NAOMIE

(a)   The answer is £Nil

(b)   The answer is £4,169

Working
(£39,000 – £8,788) × 13.8%   £4,169

(c)   The answer is £573

Working
£4,150 × 13.8%   £573

Tutorial note

Employees are not required to pay class 1 national insurance contributions once they have attained state pension age

CHARGEABLE GAINS

BASICS OF CAPITAL GAINS TAX

81   CONNECTED PERSONS

For each statement, tick the appropriate box.

	Actual proceeds used	Deemed proceeds used	No gain no loss basis
(a) Sister gives an asset to her brother		✓	
(b) Civil partner gives an asset to civil partner			✓
(c) Tareq sells an asset to his friend for £38,000. He later discovers the asset is worth £45,000.	✓		

Tutorial note

'Deemed proceeds used' is the term used by the AAT in the past.

*The term means that the **market value of the asset** will be used instead of actual sale proceeds as the starting point of the capital gain computation.*

Market value must be used where there is:

- *a disposal to a connected person (except for inter spouse and civil partnership transfers)*
- *a gift to any person*
- *sales at an undervaluation to anyone (except for inter spouse and civil partnership transfers).*

A sale at undervaluation is where an asset is deliberately/knowingly sold for less than the market value.

A bad bargain (i.e. accidentally selling for less than the asset is worth) will not be caught by special rules and the actual sale proceeds received would be used in this case. A friend is not classed as a connected person for the purposes of this legislation.

Inter spouse and civil partnership transfers are always treated as no gain/no loss transactions.

82   HARRY AND BEATRIZ

(a)   The answer is £202,000.

Working

	£
Proceeds	400,000
Less: Cost	(155,000)
Conservatory	(15,000)
Extension	(28,000)
Chargeable gain	202,000

(b)   The answer is £4,286.

Working

Cost (part disposal)	
(£10,000/£10,000 + £25,000) × £15,000	£4,286

Tutorial note

Redecoration costs are a revenue expense and are not deducted in the capital gain calculation.

The cost of the chairs sold must be found by applying the part disposal formula to the cost:

Cost × A/A + B

Where   A = gross sales proceeds, and
B = market value of the part of the asset kept.

(c)   The statement is false.

Tutorial note

Auction costs are an allowable deduction from sales proceeds.

83   SAMANTHA

	Actual proceeds used	Deemed proceeds used	No gain no loss basis
(a) Samantha sells an asset to her colleague for £8,000. She then discovers that it was worth £10,000	✓		
(b) Neil sells an asset to his wife for £10,000 when the market value is £14,000			✓
(c) Selim gives an asset to his friend.		✓	

Tutorial note

'Deemed proceeds used' is the term used by the AAT in the past.

*The term means that the **market value of the asset** will be used instead of actual sale proceeds as the starting point of the capital gain computation.*

Market value must be used where there is:

- *a disposal to a connected person (except for inter spouse and civil partnership transfers)*

- *a gift to any person*

- *sales at an undervaluation to anyone (except for inter spouse and civil partnership transfers)*

A sale at undervaluation is where an asset is deliberately / knowingly sold for less than the market value.

A bad bargain (i.e. accidentally selling for less than the asset is worth) will not be caught by special rules and the actual sale proceeds received would be used in this case.

Inter spouse and civil partnership transfers are always treated as no gain / no loss transactions.

84   JAY AND CARLI

(a)   The answer is £50,000.

	£
Proceeds	120,000
Less: Cost	(70,000)
Chargeable gain	50,000

Tutorial note

Repair costs are not capital expenditure and therefore not allowable deductions in the chargeable gains computation.

(b)   The answer is a loss of £23,500.

	£
Proceeds	30,000
Less: Selling costs – auctioneers fees (£30,000 × 5%)	(1,500)
	28,500
Less: Cost	(50,000)
Purchase costs – auctioneer's fees (£50,000 × 4%)	(2,000)
Allowable capital loss	(23,500)

(c)   The statement is false.

Tutorial note

Shares are not chattels as they are not tangible assets, and so the sale of shares which cost and are sold for less than £6,000 is chargeable.

85   VICTORIA

The answer is B.

Tutorial note

Victoria is connected with her husband Cecil, son-in-law Mike, and her sister Janet. Cousins and nieces do not meet the definition of connected persons here.

86 JOAQUIN

(a) The answer is £60,000.

	£
Proceeds	300,000
Less: Cost	(180,000)
Enhancement expenditure	(60,000)
Chargeable gain	60,000

Tutorial note

Repair costs are not capital expenditure and therefore not allowable deductions in the chargeable gains computation.

87 ESHE

The answer is £9,300.

	£	£
Necklace		
Market value	50,000	
Less: Cost	(31,400)	
Chargeable gain		18,600
Table		
Proceeds	11,000	
Less: Cost	(8,000)	
Chargeable gain		3,000
Total chargeable gains		21,600
Less: Annual exempt amount		(12,300)
Taxable gains		9,300

Tutorial note

Disposal (i) is to a connected person and so market value is automatically substituted for proceeds. Market value is also used as proceeds for disposal (ii) because it is a gift (this applies regardless of whether or not the donor and donee are connected persons). However, because Eshe is connected with the donee, the loss in disposal (ii) can only be deducted from future gains on disposals to her wife's brother and so is ignored in the calculation of taxable gains.

Eshe is not connected to her cousin so market value would only be substituted if there was a deliberate sale at undervalue. This is not the case here so the actual proceeds of £11,000 are used.

88   KAMILAH

(a)   The gain is £23,000 (£48,000 – £25,000).

Tutorial note

The destruction of an asset is a disposal with the insurance received as the proceeds figure.

(b)   The answer is £14,107.

Working

	£
Proceeds	20,000
Less: Cost £20,000/(£20,000 + £36,000) × £16,500	(5,893)
Chargeable gain	14,107

Tutorial note

The cost of the one painting sold from a set of three must be found by applying the part disposal formula to the cost:

Cost × A/A + B

Where   A = gross sales proceeds (i.e. before selling expenses)
and   B = market value of the part of the asset kept

89 ALVIN

(a) The answer is £65,564.

Working – Disposal in June 2020

	£
Proceeds (£83,000 + £2,000)	85,000
Less: Selling expenses	(2,000)
Net sales proceeds	83,000
Less: Cost £40,000 × (£85,000/£85,000 + £110,000)	(17,436)
Chargeable gain	65,564

Tutorial note

The cost of the land sold must be found by applying the part disposal formula to the cost:

Cost × A/A + B

Where   A = gross sales proceeds (i.e. before selling expenses)
and   B = market value of the part of the asset kept

Questions involving part disposals of a number of acres of land are popular with examiners. It is important to apportion the cost of the part sold using the formula and NOT the number of acres sold.

The cost of the unsold land will be the remainder of the cost.

(b) The answer is £93,936.

Working – Disposal in December 2020

	£
Proceeds	118,000
Less: Selling expenses	(1,500)
Net sales proceeds	116,500
Less: Cost (£40,000 – £17,436)	(22,564)
Chargeable gain	93,936

Tutorial note

In questions where selling costs are involved it is very important to note whether the figure provided is given net, or gross, of sales proceeds.

The figure for the sales proceeds regarding the June 2020 disposal is given net of selling costs whereas those provided for the December 2020 disposal are before deduction of selling costs.

90   REYANSH

Asset	Sale proceeds	Cost	Gain/Loss
1	£5,000	£4,000	Exempt Proceeds and cost are both < £6,000
2	£10,000	£7,000	Gain = £3,000 No special rules apply, as proceeds and cost are both > £6,000
3	£9,000	£3,000	Gain = £5,000 Gain is lower of: (£9,000 – £3,000) = £6,000, or 5/3 × (£9,000 – £6,000) = £5,000
4	£4,000	£9,000	Loss = £3,000 Deemed proceeds of £6,000 must be used

Tutorial note

The chattel marginal gain rules apply when the proceeds > £6,000 and the cost < £6,000.

The gain is taken to be the lower of

(i)   The gain calculated as normal

(ii)   5/3 × (Gross proceeds – £6,000)

Special loss rules apply when proceeds < £6,000 and the cost > £6,000.

The allowable loss is calculated assuming gross sale proceeds of £6,000.

91   CHATTELS – MARGINAL GAIN

	Applies	Does not apply
A racehorse bought for £4,000 and sold for £7,500		✓
A necklace bought for £5,900 plus £200 of auction costs, and given away when its market value was £8,000		✓
An antique vase bought for £3,000 and sold for £8,200	✓	
A painting bought for £3,000 and sold for £5,900		✓
Shares bought for £2,100 and sold for £6,900		✓

Tutorial note

Marginal gain rules only apply when a non-wasting chattel is disposed of and the proceeds are > £6,000 and the cost < £6,000.

In this question this only applies to the vase.

The racehorse is a wasting chattel and exempt.

The necklace costs more than £6,000 and has disposal proceeds of more than £6,000.

The painting is exempt as the cost and proceeds are both below £6,000.

Shares are not chattels.

92   MATCHING STATEMENTS

Asset	Sale proceeds	Cost	Statement
1	£12,000	£18,000	(iii)
2	£5,000	£6,000	(i)
3	£8,000	£4,000	(v)
4	£7,000	£6,500	(ii)
5	£5,000	£7,000	(iv)

Statements:

(i)   Exempt asset disposal

(ii)   Calculate gain as normal

(iii)   Calculate loss as normal

(iv)   Sale proceeds deemed to be £6,000

(v)   Marginal gain restriction applies

Tutorial note

Asset 2 cost exactly £6,000 and the proceeds are < £6,000.

The asset is therefore exempt as both the cost and sale proceeds are 'less than or equal to' £6,000.

93   MARTOK

	Exempt	Not exempt
A bravery medal he inherited from his father.	✓	
A quarter share in a racehorse	✓	
Antique violin sold for £150,000		✓
His personal computer	✓	
Shares held in an ISA	✓	

Tutorial note

A decoration for valour acquired other than by purchase (i.e. inherited) is specifically an exempt asset for capital gains tax purposes.

A racehorse and personal computer are wasting chattels and therefore exempt.

Although shares are not exempt as chattels, shares held in an ISA are exempt from capital gains tax when sold.

TAXATION OF SHARES

94   STRINGER LTD

Chargeable gain calculation – 2020/21	£
Proceeds (5,000 × £10)	50,000
Less: Cost (W)	(20,833)
Chargeable gain	29,167

Working: Share pool

		Number	Cost £
July 2012	Purchase (8,000 × £8)	8,000	64,000
March 2013	Purchase (4,000 × £9)	4,000	36,000
		12,000	100,000
July 2015	Sale (£100,000 × 3,000/12,000)	(3,000)	(25,000)
		9,000	75,000
May 2019	Bonus issue (1 for 1)	9,000	0
		18,000	75,000
Feb 2021	Sale (£75,000 × 5,000/18,000)	(5,000)	(20,833)
Balance c/f		13,000	54,167

Key answer tips

Remember you are only being asked to calculate the gain on the February 2021 disposal. The July 2015 disposal is only important for the pool calculation. The sales proceeds at this date are irrelevant here.

The disposal in July 2015 will reduce the balance of the pool for the later disposal so calculate the cost of the share sold in the usual way then add down to give the balance to carry forward.

You are also asked for the chargeable gain, not the taxable gain; therefore do not waste time deducting the annual exempt amount.

95   LULU LTD

Chargeable gain calculation

	£
Proceeds (8,000 × £7)	56,000
Less: Cost (W)	(29,538)
Chargeable gain	26,462

Working: Share pool

		Number	Cost £
Oct 2010	Purchase (12,000 × £4)	12,000	48,000
June 2012	Bonus 1 for 12	1,000	0
		13,000	48,000
April 2016	Sale (£48,000 × 3,000/13,000)	(3,000)	(11,077)
		10,000	36,923
Jan 2021	Sale (£36,923 × 8,000/10,000)	(8,000)	(29,538)
Balance c/f		2,000	7,385

Key answer tips

Remember you are only being asked to calculate the gain on the January 2021 disposal. The April 2016 disposal is only important for the pool calculation. The sales proceeds at this date are irrelevant here.

The disposal in April 2016 will reduce the balance of the pool for the later disposal so calculate the cost of the share sold in the usual way then add down to give the balance to carry forward.

You are also asked for the chargeable gain, not the taxable gain; therefore do not waste time deducting the annual exempt amount.

96   GILBERT LTD

Chargeable gain calculation

		£
1	On 1,200 shares matched with the 15 September 2020 purchase	
	Proceeds 1,200/8,000 × £65,000	9,750
	Less: Cost	(9,600)
	Chargeable gain	150
2	On 1,200 shares matched with the 18 September 2020 purchase	
	Proceeds 1,000/8,000 × £65,000	8,125
	Less: Cost	(10,000)
	Loss	(1,875)
3	On 5,800 shares matched with the pool	
	Proceeds (£65,000 – £9,750 - £8,125))	47,125
	Less: Cost (W)	(23,200)
	Chargeable gain	23,925
	Total gain (£23,925 +£150 - £1,875)	22,200

Working: Share pool

		Number	Cost £
May 2009	Purchase (8,000 × £4)	8,000	32,000
June 2013	Bonus 1 for 4	2,000	0
July 2015	Purchase (2,000 × £8)	2,000	16,000
		12,000	48,000
Sept 2020	Sale (£48,000 × 5,800/12,000)	(5,800)	(23,200)
Balance c/f		6,200	24,800

Tutorial note

In relation to individuals, we match shares disposed of in the following order:

- *first, with shares acquired on the same day as the disposal*
- *second, with shares acquired within the following 30 days (using the earliest acquisition first, i.e. on a FIFO basis)*
- *third, with the share pool (all the shares bought before the date of disposal).*

In this case there are 1,200 shares purchased on 15 September 2020 and 1,000 purchased on 18 September 2020, both of which are within 30 days after the disposal on 7 September 2020. Hence 1,200 of the shares sold on 7 September are matched with the purchase on 15 September, and then 1,000 shares are matched with the purchase on 18 September.

The remaining 5,800 shares sold are matched with the share pool.

97   BELLA

Chargeable gain calculation

		£
1	On 1,000 shares matched with the 17 May 2020 purchase	
	Proceeds (1,000 × £11)	11,000
	Less: Cost (1,000 × £10)	(10,000)
	Chargeable gain	1,000
2	On pool shares	
	Proceeds (8,000 × £11)	88,000
	Less: Cost (W)	(46,222)
	Chargeable gain	41,778
	Total gain (£1,000 + £41,778)	42,778

Working: Share pool

		Number	Cost £
Sept 2012	Purchase (16,000 × £6)	16,000	96,000
June 2016	Rights issue 1 for 8 (2,000 × £4)	2,000	8,000
		18,000	104,000
May 2020	Sale (£104,000 × 8,000/18,000)	(8,000)	(46,222)
Balance c/f		10,000	57,778

Tutorial note

In relation to individuals, we match shares disposed of in the following order:

- *first, with shares acquired on the same day as the disposal*

- *second, with shares acquired within the following 30 days (using the earliest acquisition first, i.e. on a FIFO basis)*

- *third, with the share pool (all the shares bought before the date of disposal).*

In this case there are 1,000 shares purchased on 17 May 2020 which is within 30 days after the disposal on 14 May 2020. Hence 1,000 of the shares sold on 14 May are matched with the purchase on 17 May.

The remaining 8,000 shares sold are matched with the share pool.

98 BAJOR PLC

Chargeable gain calculation

	£
Proceeds	17,500
Less: Cost (W)	(9,035)
Chargeable gain	8,465

Working: Share pool

		Number	Cost £
Feb 2010	Purchase	2,000	7,560
July 2012	Bonus 1 for 10	200	0
Dec 2014	Purchase	500	2,800
		2,700	10,360
Apr 2016	Rights issue (1 for 5) at £2.50	540	1,350
		3,240	11,710
Mar 2021	Sale (£11,710 × 2,500/3,240)	(2,500)	(9,035)
Balance c/f		740	2,675

99   ASPEN LTD

Chargeable gain calculation

			£
1	On 200 shares matched with the 18 June 2020 purchase		
	Proceeds (200 × £6)		1,200
	Less: Cost (200 × £5.5)		(1,100)
	Chargeable gain		100
2	On 400 shares matched with the 25 June 2020 purchase		
	Proceeds (400 × £6)		2,400
	Less: Cost (400 × £7)		(2,800)
	Loss		(400)
3	On 1,400 shares matched with the pool		
	Proceeds (1,400 × £6)		8,400
	Less: Cost (W)		(4,667)
	Chargeable gain		3,733
	Total gain (£3,733 + £100 - £400)		3,433

Working: Share pool

		Number	Cost £
Nov 2016	Purchase (4,000 × £5)	4,000	20,000
July 2018	Bonus 1 for 2	2,000	0
		6,000	20,000
Sept 2020	Sale (£20,000 × 1,400/6,000)	(1,400)	(4,667)
Balance c/f		4,600	15,333

Tutorial note

In relation to individuals, we match shares disposed of in the following order:

- first, with shares acquired on the same day as the disposal
- second, with shares acquired within the following 30 days (using the earliest acquisition first, i.e. on a FIFO basis)
- third, with the share pool (all the shares bought before the date of disposal).

In this case there are 200 shares purchased on the date of disposal so we match with these first. We then have 400 purchased on 25 June 2020, which is within 30 days after the disposal on 18 June 2020. Hence 400 of the shares sold on 18 June are matched with the purchase on 25 June.

The remaining 1,400 shares sold are matched with the share pool.

CAPITAL GAINS TAX EXEMPTIONS, LOSSES, RELIEFS, TAX PAYABLE

100   AGUSTIN

The answer is £722.

Working

Capital gains tax payable computation – 2020/21

	£
Gross sale proceeds	25,927
Less: Selling costs (2% × £25,927)	(519)
Net sale proceeds	25,408
Less: Cost	(8,000)
Chargeable gain	17,408
Less: Annual exempt amount	(12,300)
Taxable gain	5,108

Capital gains tax:	
£	
3,000 × 10% (W)	300
2,108 × 20%	422
─────	
5,108	
─────	
Capital gains tax payable	722

Remaining basic rate band

	£
Basic rate band	37,500
Less: Taxable income (£47,000 – £12,500)	(34,500)
Remaining basic rate band	3,000

Tutorial note

The taxable income falls below the basic rate band threshold, therefore there is some of the basic rate band remaining to match against the taxable gains.

Taxable gains fall partly into the remaining basic rate band and partly into the higher rate band. The capital gains tax liability is therefore calculated in two parts at 10% and 20%.

101 ANGELA

The answer is £18,445.

Working

Capital gains tax computation – 2020/21

	£
Sale proceeds	290,000
Less: Cost	(150,000)
Enhancement expenditure	(29,700)
Chargeable gain	110,300
Less: Annual exempt amount	(12,300)
Taxable gains	98,000

Capital gains tax:

£	
11,555 × 10% (W)	1,156
86,445 × 20%	17,289
98,000	
Capital gains tax payable	18,445

Remaining basic rate band

	£
Basic rate band	37,500
Plus: Gift aid donation (£400 × 100/80)	500
Extended basic rate band	38,000
Less: Taxable income	(26,445)
Remaining basic rate band	11,555

Tutorial note

The taxable income falls below the basic rate band threshold, therefore there is some of the basic rate band remaining to match against the taxable gains.

However, be careful as the basic rate band will be extended by the gross gift aid donation.

Taxable gains fall partly into the remaining basic rate band and partly into the higher rate band. The capital gains tax liability is therefore calculated in two parts at 10% and 20%.

102 KIESWETTER

(a) The statement is true.

Tutorial note

For the purposes of the AAT assessment, all animals including greyhounds, racehorses, etc., are wasting chattels, so they are exempt assets.

(b) The statement is false.

Tutorial note

Cars are always exempt assets.

(c) The answer is B.

Working

	£
Capital gains for the year	20,300
Less: Capital losses for the year	(4,500)
Net gains	15,800
Less: Annual exempt amount	(12,300)
	3,500
Less: Capital losses brought forward (restricted)	(3,500)
Taxable gains	0

Capital losses carried forward are £3,200 (£6,700 b/f − £3,500 used)

Tutorial note

All current year losses must be set against current year capital gains, even if they waste the annual exempt amount.

Capital losses brought forward are used after the annual exempt and their use is restricted to the amount needed to bring taxable gains down to nil.

103 JOANNA

	True	False
Capital gains are taxed at 10% for all taxpayers.		✓
If a taxpayer does not use their annual exempt amount in 2019/20 they can bring it forward to use in 2020/21.		✓
The use of brought forward capital losses is made after the annual exempt amount.	✓	

Tutorial note

The rate of capital gains tax depends on the level of the taxable income.

Taxable gains are taxed after taxable income.

Taxable gains falling into the basic rate band are taxed at 10%. Those gains falling into the higher rate band are taxed at 20%.

If a taxpayer does not use his annual exempt amount for capital gains tax purposes, it cannot be carried forward or backwards and it cannot be given away. It is wasted (i.e. lost).

104 ALYSHA

	£
Proceeds	52,000
Less: Selling costs – auctioneers fees (£52,000 × 2%)	(1,040)
	50,960
Less: Cost	(35,300)
Purchase costs – legal fees	(250)
Chargeable gain	15,410
Less: Annual exempt amount	(12,300)
Taxable gain	3,110
Capital gains tax (£3,110 × 20%)	622

Tutorial note

Accountant's fees for preparing a capital gains tax computation are not an allowable cost for capital gain purposes.

Capital gains tax is calculated at 20% as Alysha is a higher rate taxpayer.

105 KEVIN

The answer is C.

Tutorial note

Only the annual exempt amount can be deducted from chargeable gains, the personal allowance can only be deducted from income.

Current year capital losses are offset before the annual exempt amount and cannot be restricted to preserve it.

106 RASHIDA

	Capital loss b/f £	Chargeable gain 2020/21 £	Capital loss 2020/21 £	Capital loss c/f (workings below) £
1	7,560	25,000	11,290	6,150
2	0	16,500	21,000	4,500
3	12,900	14,780	8,000	12,900
4	5,200	13,800	0	3,700

Workings

		£
(W1)	Chargeable gains for the year	25,000
	Less: Capital losses for the year	(11,290)
		———
	Net gains	13,710
	Less: Annual exempt amount	(12,300)
		———
		1,410
	Less: Capital losses brought forward (restricted)	(1,410)
		———
	Taxable gains	0
		———

Capital losses carried forward are £6,150 (£7,560 b/f – £1,410 used)

		£
(W2)	Chargeable gains for the year	16,500
	Less: Capital losses for the year	(21,000)
		———
	Net loss c/f	(4,500)
		———

		£
(W3)	Chargeable gains for the year	14,780
	Less: Capital losses for the year	(8,000)
	Net gains	6,780
	Less: Annual exempt amount (restricted)	(6,780)
	Less: Capital losses brought forward	(0)
	Taxable gains	0

Capital losses carried forward are £12,900

		£
(W4)	Chargeable gains for the year	13,800
	Less: Capital losses for the year	0
	Net gains	13,800
	Less: Annual exempt amount	(12,300)
		1,500
	Less: Capital losses brought forward (restricted)	(1,500)
	Taxable gains	0

Capital losses carried forward are £3,700 (£5,200 b/f – £1,500 used)

> *Tutorial note*
>
> *All current year losses must be set against current year capital gains, even if they waste the annual exempt amount.*
>
> *However, when capital losses are brought forward, they are offset after the annual exempt amount, meaning their use does not lead to this being wasted.*

107 ARLENE

	£
Gains	31,900
Capital losses	(4,100)
	27,800
Less: Annual exempt amount	(12,300)
Taxable gains	15,500

	£		
	7,200	× 10%	720
(£15,500 − £7,200)	8,300	× 20%	1,660
	15,500		2,380

Due date of payment   31.1.2022

108   HUEY, DUEY AND LOUIE

Taxpayer	Net gains 2020/21	Loss 2019/20 b/f	Relieve all loss	Relieve some loss	Relieve no loss
Huey	£21,750	£6,550	✓		
Duey	£10,530	£5,150			✓
Louie	£15,090	£7,820		✓	

Tutorial note

Capital losses brought forward are only used to reduce the net gains for the year down to the level of the annual exempt amount.

109   TINEKE

Occupation	Non-occupation
1 June 2012 – 31 Dec 2012	
1 Jan 2013 – 31 Dec 2014 (working abroad)	
1 Jan 2015 – 31 Aug 2015 (working away in UK)	
1 Sep 2015 – 30 Nov 2015	1 Dec 2015 – 31 March 2020
1 Apr 2020 – 31 Dec 2020 (Last 9 months)	

Tutorial note

A taxpayer's private residence is exempt for the periods when it is occupied or deemed occupied.

The last nine months of ownership are always deemed occupation even if the taxpayer has another residence by then.

> *Other deemed residence periods:*
>
> *(i)   Any period working abroad – this covers Tineke's two years abroad.*
>
> *(ii)   Up to a total of 4 years working elsewhere in the UK – this covers Tineke's eight months working away in the UK.*
>
> *(iii) Up to a total of 3 years for any reason.*
>
> *These periods must be preceded at some time by actual occupation and followed by actual occupation (except occupation after the absence is not insisted on for (i) and (ii) if the taxpayer cannot return to their residence due to being moved elsewhere to work).*
>
> *This means that the 3 years for any reason cannot be applied to the time Tineke lives with her boyfriend as she does not return to the flat.*

110   RENATA

Occupation	Non-occupation
1 May 2010 – 31 Dec 2013	1 Jan 2014 – 30 Sept 2019
1 Oct 2019 – 30 Jun 2020 (Last nine months)	

Tutorial note

A taxpayer's private residence is exempt for the periods when it is occupied or deemed occupied.

The last nine months of ownership are always deemed occupation even if the taxpayer has another residence by then.

This is the only period of deemed occupation allowed as Renata does not work abroad, nor elsewhere in the UK and the 3 years for any reason cannot be applied to the time Renata lives with her sister as she does not return to the flat.

111   YASMIN

	All treated as occupation	Part treated as occupation	Not treated as occupation
(a) Yasmin spent 10 years working abroad.	✓		
(b) George spent 4 years motorcycling around the world.		✓	
(c) The last 4 years of Owen's ownership in which he did not live in the house.		✓	
(d) Ian spent 5 years working elsewhere in the UK	✓		

(e)	Irina moved out of her house and spent 2 years living in her boyfriend's house. After they split up she moved back to live with her parents and never moved back to her own house which she sold 5 years later.		
	– for the 2 years living with boyfriend		✓
	– for the 5 years living with parents	✓	

Tutorial note

The last nine months of ownership are always deemed occupation even if the taxpayer has another residence by then.

Other deemed residence periods:

(i)   Any period working abroad

(ii)   Up to a total of 4 years working elsewhere in the UK.

(iii) Up to a total of 3 years for any reason.

These periods must be preceded at some time by actual occupation and followed by actual occupation (except occupation after the absence is not insisted on for (i) and (ii) if the taxpayer cannot return to their residence due to being moved elsewhere to work.)

Yasmin is covered by (i).

George is not covered by (i) as he is not working, however he can claim (iii) and exempt some of the period of absence.

Owen's last 4 years is partly covered by the last nine months rule.

Ian is covered by (ii) and the last year by (iii).

Irina's 2 years living with her boyfriend are not covered as she does not reoccupy the property at any time after the period of absence.

Irina's 5 years living with parents is partly covered by the last nine months rule.

112   ESME

(a)	The total period of ownership of the house is (in months)	120
(b)	The period of actual and deemed residence is (in months)	66
(c)	The chargeable gain on the sale of the house is	£104,125

Workings

(W1) Total ownership

The house is owned from 1 July 2010 to 30 June 2020 = 10 years or 120 months

(W2) Periods of residence and deemed residence

Residence and deemed residence	Mths	Non-occupation	Mths
1 Jul 2010 – 30 Jun 2012	24		
1 Jul 2012 – 30 Jun 2013 (Part of 3 years any reason)	12		
1 Jul 2013 – 30 Jun 2015	24	1 Jul 2015 – 31 Sept 2019	51
1 Oct 2020 – 30 Jun 2020 (Last nine months)	9		
Total	69		51

(W3) Capital gain on sale of house

	£
Proceeds	285,000
Less: Cost	(40,000)
	245,000
Less: PRR 69/120 × £245,000	(140,875)
Chargeable gain	104,125

Tutorial note

The last nine months of ownership are always deemed occupation even if the taxpayer has another residence by then.

Other deemed residence periods:

(i) Any period working abroad

(ii) Up to a total of 4 years working elsewhere in the UK.

(iii) Up to a total of 3 years for any reason.

These periods must be preceded at some time by actual occupation and followed by actual occupation (except occupation after the absence is not insisted on for (i) and (ii) if the taxpayer cannot return to their residence due to being moved elsewhere to work.)

Esme cannot claim the 'working abroad' period as deemed occupation as she was not working. However, she is always entitled to the last nine months and the period abroad can be covered by 3 years for any reason rule.

The remainder of the 3 years for any reason cannot be used to cover the period while living with her boyfriend as she does not reoccupy the property at any time after the period of absence.

---

113 LYNNETTE

Lynnette is away from her house for 12 years and never returns.

As she cannot return to her house because of her job, she can claim deemed occupation for 4 years working elsewhere in the UK. However, she cannot have the 3 years for any reason as she does not return to the house.

The last nine months of ownership are always deemed occupation.

Total occupation plus deemed occupation is 12.75 years out of the 20 owned.

	£
Capital gain	360,000
Less: Principal private residence exemption (360,000 x 12.75/20)	(229,500)
Chargeable gain	130,500

INHERITANCE TAX

114 TRANSFERS AND EXEMPTIONS (1)

	True	False
The annual exemption can be carried forward for one year but cannot be used until the annual exemption for the current year has been used.	✓	
An exempt transfer may give rise to an inheritance tax liability if the donor dies within seven years.		✓
Chargeable lifetime transfers may give rise to two separate liabilities to inheritance tax.	✓	

Tutorial note

The second statement is false because there cannot be an inheritance tax liability where a transfer is exempt. It is a potentially exempt transfer which may give rise to an inheritance tax liability if the donor dies within seven years.

The third statement is true because there may be a charge at the time of the gift and a further charge if the donor dies within seven years.

115 SAGAN

Sagan

The answer is £10,650.

Working	£
Gift	20,000
Marriage exemption from parent	(5,000)
Annual exemption 2020/21 (£3,000 – £1,650)	(1,350)
Annual exemption 2019/20 b/f	(3,000)
Chargeable amount	10,650

Yates

The answer is £1,000.

Working	£
Gift	4,100
Annual exemption 2020/21 (£3,000 – £1,800)	(1,200)
Annual exemption 2019/20 b/f (£3,000 – £1,100)	(1,900)
Chargeable amount	1,000

Porte

The answer is £2,270.

Working	£
Gift	8,000
Annual exemption 2020/21 (£3,000 – £270)	(2,730)
Annual exemption 2019/20 b/f	(3,000)
Chargeable amount	2,270

Tutorial note

The annual exemption is carried forward for one year. The current year's annual exemption must be used before using any amount brought forward.

Porte's gift on 1 June 2019 was less than £250 and would have been covered by the small gifts exemption, as it was Porte's only gift to her brother in the 2019/20 tax year. The small gifts exemption only applies if the total gifts to one person do not exceed £250 in the tax year.

---

116 SHARON

Lifetime gift

	Not exempt	Partly exempt £	Fully exempt £
1 £310 from Sharon to her husband.			✓
2 A house worth £510,000 to a trust.	✓		
3 £4,000 from Maysoun to her grandson on his wedding day.		✓	

Tutorial note

1   This gift would be covered by the spouse exemption.

2   There are no exemptions available in respect of this gift.

3   The marriage exemption of £2,500 would be available in respect of this gift.

117 TRANSFERS AND EXEMPTIONS (2)

	True	False
The small gifts exemption is £250 per donor per tax year.		✓
No inheritance tax liability can arise in respect of a gift made more than seven years prior to death.		✓
An individual who has always lived in America and is not domiciled in the UK may still be liable to pay inheritance tax in the UK.	✓	

Tutorial note

*The first statement is false because the exemption is per **donee** and not per donor.*

The second statement is false because an inheritance tax liability can arise in respect of a chargeable lifetime transfer at any time in a donor's lifetime.

The third statement is true because a person who is not domiciled in the UK may still be subject to UK inheritance tax in respect of assets situated in the UK.

118 FROOME

Froome

The answer is £1,250.

Working	£
Gift	8,250
Marriage exemption	(1,000)
Annual exemption 2020/21	(3,000)
Annual exemption 2019/20 b/f	(3,000)
Chargeable amount	1,250

Mollema

The answer is £26,600.

Working	£
Gift	32,600
Annual exemption 2020/21	(3,000)
Annual exemption 2019/20 b/f	(3,000)
Chargeable amount	26,600

Cavendish

The answer is £Nil.

The gift is covered by the small gifts exemption

Tutorial note

The annual exemption is carried forward for one year. The current year's annual exemption must be used before using any amount brought forward.

Froome's gift on 1 March 2020 was less than £250 and would have been covered by the small gifts exemption. This exemption applies if total gifts to that recipient do not exceed £250 in the tax year.

Cavendish's gift was less than £250 and would be covered by the small gifts exemption.

119 ERIC

Gift	Not exempt	Partly exempt £	Fully exempt £
1 A statue worth £830,000 from Eric to a national museum.			✓
2 A painting worth £11,500 from Gomez to his wife.			✓
3 £750 from Janine to her son.	✓		

Tutorial note

1   This gift would be covered by the exemption in respect of gifts to museums and art galleries.

2   This gift would be covered by the spouse exemption.

3   There are no exemptions available in respect of this gift.

120 TRANSFERS AND EXEMPTIONS (3)

	True	False
Lifetime inheritance tax is charged at 25% on a chargeable lifetime transfer where the donor is paying the tax.	✓	
An individual who is domiciled outside the UK is liable to inheritance tax in respect of their worldwide assets.		✓
The annual exemption can be carried forward for one year and must be used before the annual exemption for the current year.		✓

Tutorial note

The second statement is false because an individual who is domiciled outside the UK is liable to inheritance tax in respect of their UK assets only.

The third statement is false because the current annual exemption must be used before any amount brought forward.

121 ROWENA

(a) Complete the following sentences using one of the words on the right.

1 Rowena is domiciled in the UK. She owns a house situated in Australia worth £720,000.

The house .... be subject to inheritance tax in the UK when Rowena dies.

will	will not
✓	

2 Ori gave £30,000 to his niece on 1 July 2012. In September 2020 Ori died.

The gift of £30,000 .... be subject to inheritance tax on Ori's death.

may	will not
	✓

3 Umar gave £2,600 to his brother on 1 July 2018. This was his only gift in 2018/19. Umar died on 1 December 2020.

The gift of £2,600 .... be subject to inheritance tax on Umar's death.

may	will not
	✓

Tutorial note

1 *Rowena is domiciled in the UK and will therefore be subject to UK inheritance tax on her assets where ever they are situated in the world.*

2 *Ori's gift will not be subject to inheritance tax because he did not die within seven years of making it.*

3 *Umar's gift will be covered by his annual exemption for 2018/19.*

(b) Are the following statements true or false in connection with inheritance tax?

	True	False
Taper relief will reduce a transfer of value made more than three but less than seven years prior to the donor's death.		✓
Where the donor of a potentially exempt transfer dies within seven years of making the gift, any inheritance tax due is payable by the donee.	✓	

Tutorial note

The first statement is false because taper relief reduces the inheritance tax due and not the transfer of value.

122 FLORENCE

(a)   Complete the following sentences using the words on the right.

	may	will not
1 Florence gave a house worth £430,000 to her son on 1 October 2013. Florence died on 1 May 2020. The house .... be subject to inheritance tax in the UK following the death of Florence.	✓	

	would	would not
2 Jemima gave £370,000 to a trust on 1 September 2011. In June 2020 Jemima died. Inheritance tax .... have been charged on the gift when it was made.	✓	

	will	will not
3 Joshua is domiciled in France. He owns a house situated in the UK worth £675,000. This house .... be subject to inheritance tax in the UK when Joshua dies.	✓	

Tutorial note

1   *Florence's gift will be chargeable to inheritance tax because she died within seven years of making it. However, it could be covered by the nil rate band, if both Florence's nil rate band and that of a deceased spouse were available. There is not enough information in the question to confirm this. Florence's residence nil rate band will not be available to set against this gift, as it was not left in her death estate.*

2   *A gift to a trust is a chargeable lifetime transfer. This gift exceeds the nil rate band and would have been subject to inheritance tax when it was made.*

3   *Joshua's house is situated in the UK and will be subject to UK inheritance tax regardless of where Joshua is domiciled.*

(b)   Are the following statements true or false in connection with inheritance tax?

	True	False
The inheritance tax due in respect of the residue of a death estate is paid by the residuary legatee.		✓
The annual exemption cannot be deducted from the death estate even if there have been no gifts in the year of death.	✓	

Tutorial note

*The first statement is false because, although the inheritance tax due in respect of the residue of a death estate is **suffered** by the residuary legatee, it is **paid** by the personal representatives.*

123 ADI

The answer is £54,750.

Working	£	£
Gift – gross chargeable transfer		511,250
Nil rate band	325,000	
Gross chargeable transfers in the seven years prior to the gift	(270,000)	
Nil rate band available		(55,000)
Chargeable amount		456,250
Inheritance tax (£456,250 × 40%)		182,500
Taper relief (£182,500 × 20%) (3-4 years between gift and death)		(36,500)
		146,000
Inheritance tax paid during lifetime		(91,250)
Further inheritance tax due on death		54,750

Tutorial note

Taper relief is available on any gift made more than three years before death. The amount of relief depends on how many years have passed between the date of the gift and the date of death and these rates are in the tax tables available to you in the assessment. There have been more than three years and less than four years between the date of the gift and the date of death, therefore there is a 20% reduction in the inheritance tax.

124   BERNARD

The answer is £146,000.

Working	£	£
Value of estate		1,600,000
Legacy to wife – spouse exemption		(800,000)
Legacy to charity – exemption		(20,000)
Gross chargeable estate		780,000
Residence nil rate band		(175,000)
Nil rate band	325,000	
Gross chargeable transfers in the seven years prior to death	(85,000)	
Nil rate band available		(240,000)
Taxable amount		365,000
Inheritance tax (£365,000 × 40%)		146,000

Tutorial note

The residence nil rate band (RNRB) of £175,000 is available as Bernard has left a residential property that he has lived in to his direct descendants. As the value of that property was greater than the RNRB, it is available in full. He is not entitled to a transferred NRB or RNRB from his wife as she is still alive.

125   CAMPION

The answer is £15,600.

Working	£	£
Gift after deduction of all exemptions		200,000
Nil rate band	325,000	
Gross chargeable transfers in the seven years prior to the gift	(190,000)	
Nil rate band available		(135,000)
Chargeable amount		65,000
Inheritance tax (£65,000 × 40%)		26,000
Taper relief (£26,000 × 40%) (4–5 years between gift and death)		(10,400)
Inheritance tax due on death		15,600

Tutorial note

Taper relief is available on any gift made more than three years before death. The amount of relief depends on how many years have passed between the date of the gift and the date of death and these rates are in the tax tables available to you in the assessment. There have been more than four years and less than five years between the date of the gift and the date of death, therefore there is a 40% reduction in the inheritance tax.

126 DESDEMONA

The answer is £398,600.

Working	£	£
Value of estate		1,300,000
Nil rate band	325,000	
Nil rate band transferred from husband (£325,000 × 38%)	123,500	
Gross chargeable transfers in the seven years prior to death	(145,000)	
Nil rate band available		(303,500)
Taxable amount		996,500
Inheritance tax (£996,500 × 40%)		398,600

127 EMILE

The answer is £21,000.

Working	£	£
Gift after deduction of all exemptions		350,000
Nil rate band	325,000	
Gross chargeable transfers in the seven years prior to the gift	(80,000)	
Nil rate band available		(245,000)
Chargeable amount		105,000
Inheritance tax (£105,000 × 20%)		21,000

Tutorial note

Inheritance tax is payable at 20% on a chargeable lifetime transfer when the trustees agree to pay the tax due. If the tax was paid by the donor it would be charged at 25%.

128 FOTHERINGTON

(a)   The answer is £Nil

> **Working**
>
> | | £ | £ |
> |---|---|---|
> | Gift after deduction of all exemptions | | 45,000 |
> | Nil rate band | | (325,000) |
> | Chargeable amount | | 0 |
> | Inheritance tax | | 0 |

(b)   The answer is £545,200.

> **Working**
>
> | | £ | £ |
> |---|---|---|
> | Value of estate | | 1,750,000 |
> | Residence nil rate band (lower of property value and £150,000) | | (107,000) |
> | Nil rate band | 325,000 | |
> | Gross chargeable transfers in the seven years prior to death | (45,000) | |
> | Nil rate band available | | (280,000) |
> | Taxable amount | | 1,363,000 |
> | Inheritance tax (£1,363,000 × 40%) | | 545,200 |

Section 3

MOCK ASSESSMENT QUESTIONS

TASK 1 (10 marks)

You work for a firm of accountants and are in the process of preparing the 2020/21 tax return for Thelma, one of your clients. Thelma has received dividends from a number of companies during the year. However, she has not provided you with the relevant information. She stated that 'the amounts involved were immaterial and that it wasn't worth sorting out the details'.

Using the AAT guidelines 'Professional conduct in relation to taxation', explain your responsibilities in relation to this matter. **(10 marks)**

TASK 2 (8 marks)

Mandeep was unemployed until 6 June 2020, when he started a new job as a salesman.

As part of his remuneration package, he was provided with the following benefits:

- From 6 November 2020, a Ford car. The list price of the car is £15,000 and Mandeep paid his company £100 per month in respect of his private use of the car. This car was registered after 6 April 2020.

- The CO_2 emissions are 118 g/km and it has a diesel engine. The car does not meet the RDE2 requirements.

- The company pays for all the running costs of the car including the fuel. Mandeep paid his company £30 per month towards the provision of diesel.

- From 6 December 2020, a Peugeot car for his wife. The list price of the car is £12,000; however, the company bought it for £10,000. This car was registered before 6 April 2020. The CO_2 emissions are 29 g/km and the car has an electric range of 39 miles.

- It has a petrol hybrid engine; but the company does not pay for any private fuel on this car.

Complete the following in relation to Mandeep's taxable benefits in respect of the provision of the cars and fuel. **(8 marks)**

(i)	What is the appropriate percentage for Mandeep's Ford car?	%
(ii)	What is the taxable benefit for the use of the Ford car?	£
(iii)	What is the taxable benefit for the fuel provided by the company?	£
(iv)	What is the appropriate percentage for Mandeep's wife's car?	%
(v)	What price is used to calculate the car benefit on Mandeep's wife's car?	£
(vi)	What is the taxable benefit for Mandeep's wife's car?	£
(vii)	On 6 April 2021 accessories of £90 were added to Mandeep's ford car. What price is used to calculate the car benefit for Mandeep for 2021/22?	£

TASK 3 (8 marks)

(a) What is the taxable benefit for each of the employment benefits received by the employees listed below? **(5 marks)**

(i)	Carol's employer paid £6,700 to cover the costs she incurred when she relocated from Newcastle to Hull in order to start work in her new job.	£
(ii)	Bill received £1,800 as a loan from his employer throughout 2020/21. He pays interest on the loan at the rate of 2%.	£
(iii)	Les borrowed a digital camera from his employer on 6 June 2020 until 5 April 2021 to use on his holidays and for family occasions. The market value of the camera on 6 June 2020 was £1,200.	£
(iv)	From 6 January 2021, Farah was provided with a company loan of £22,000 on which she pays interest at 1.50% per annum.	£
(v)	Majid was provided with accommodation by his employer. The house has an annual value £4,200 and the employer pays a rent of £250 per month. His employer also paid a utility bill for the house of £180 during 2020/21. Majid moved out when he left his employment on 5 December 2020.	£

(b) Rose has asked you to advise her which of the following benefits are exempt. Tick the relevant box on each line. **(3 marks)**

	Exempt	Not exempt
Private use of a company car that was first registered on 6 April 2020 with CO_2 emissions of 52 g/km		
A place in the company's workplace based nursery for two children		
A second mobile telephone for the spouse of each employee		
Provision of bicycle helmets for staff earning below £20,000 p.a.		
Staff Christmas party costing £75 per employee		
Relocation expenses of £7,500		

TASK 4 (6 marks)

(a)   **Mark the following statements as true or false**   **(3 marks)**

	True	False
Income tax is always charged at 0% on the first £2,000 of a taxpayer's dividend income.		
An individual who receives annual pension income of £19,000, will pay income tax of £1,200 on savings income of £6,000 in 2020/21.		
A higher rate taxpayer receives interest from an ISA of £600. The £600 received is exempt from income tax.		

(b)   **Calculate the total tax payable by the following individuals in respect of their investment income in 2020/21.**   **(3 marks)**

	Total tax payable on investment income
Polly earned an annual salary of £88,000 and received savings income of £6,700.	
Priscilla received dividend income of £6,100. She also received an annual salary of £172,000.	
Priti received interest income from a bank of £1,500. She also has employment income of £149,000.	

TASK 5 (6 marks)

Steven has three properties, details of which are as follows:

Four-bedroom house:

1   This furnished house is rented out for £780 per month. The property was occupied throughout 2020/21.

2   Steven sold the dining furniture in this property for £160 in October 2020. He chose to purchase higher quality furniture costing £2,700 rather than furniture of a similar quality that would have cost £2,200.

3   The only other expense paid by Steven in respect of the house was 7% commission to the agent on the rent received.

One bedroom flat:

4   This unfurnished flat is rented out for £415 per month. The property was occupied until 5 October 2020 when the tenants moved out without paying the last month's rent. It is highly unlikely that Steven will be able to recover this debt. New tenants moved in on 6 January 2021 when the rent had increased to £435 per month.

5   Steven paid a cleaner £60 per month to clean this property throughout 2020/21; however, the last month's payment was not made until 10 April 2020.

Two-bedroom house:

6   This house was rented out from 6 July 2020 for £610 per month.

7   Steven paid £280 on 28 March 2021 for roof repairs that were carried out in the last week of April 2021.

All amounts were paid / received during the tax year 2020/21 unless indicated otherwise.

Calculate the profit or loss made on each property using the following table.

Do not use brackets or minus signs and if you feel any items are not allowable please insert a zero '0'.   **(6 marks)**

	Four bedroom house £	One bedroom flat £	Two bedroom house £
Income			
Expenses:			
Dining furniture			
Commission			
Cleaning			
Furniture			
Roof repairs			
Profit or Loss			

TASK 6 (12 marks)

Rita is employed as a receptionist with a gross annual salary of £33,030. On 21 April 2020, she received a bonus of £4,435 which related to her performance during the year ended 31 March 2020. She has paid £4,993 of PAYE during the year.

Rita received dividends of £13,025 and ISA interest of £6,980

Enter your answer and workings into the table below to calculate Rita's income tax payable for 2020/21. Show the answer in whole pounds. **(12 marks)**

TASK 7 (4 marks)

Laura is 41 years old and is employed by Plyo Ltd. In 2020/21 Laura received the following from her employer:

	£
Salary	73,000
Workplace childcare costing Plyo Ltd	2,800
Benefit in respect of company car	7,700

Laura incurred expenses of £5,120 wholly, exclusively and necessarily in the performance of her duties.

(a)   **What is Laura's liability to class 1 national insurance contributions for 2020/21 in pounds and pence?**   **(2 marks)**

(b)   **What is Plyo Ltd.'s liability to class 1 national insurance contributions for 2020/21 in respect of Laura in pounds and pence?**   **(1 mark)**

(c)   **What is Plyo Ltd.'s liability to class 1A national insurance contributions for 2020/21 in respect of Laura in pounds and pence?**   **(1 mark)**

TASK 8 (7 marks)

(a)   Today's date is 1 April 2020.

Niamh is a higher rate taxpayer, and also earns £500 of savings income a year.

She has just inherited £300,000 from her uncle, and is considering how to invest the funds. She does not wish to invest in shares, as she considers this risky. Instead, she is considering investing the money in a bank deposit account, which will earn approximately £9,000 of interest during 2020/21 at an average of 3%.

Alternatively, Niamh may consider investing in other types of bank account and/or transferring some or all of her inheritance to her husband Roberto for him to invest instead.

You should assume that any investments made will earn 3% interest per annum.

Roberto has taxable income of £30,500, which is all employment income.

(a)   (i)   To the nearest pound, how much tax will the couple save if both she and Roberto invest the maximum amount each in an ISA rather than a standard bank account?   **(2 marks)**

(ii)   To the nearest pound, how much tax will the couple save by if Niamh transfers sufficient funds to Roberto to utilise his savings allowance for 2020/21?

(1 marks)

(iii)   To the nearest pound, how much tax will the couple save if in addition to point (ii) above the rest of the funds are transferred to Roberto before investment in the bank deposit account ?   **(2 marks)**

(b)   Mark the following statement as true or false   **(2 marks)**

	True	False
There is no upper limit on the amount of tax-free chargeable gains which can be made by a taxpayer in a tax year in respect of shares held in an ISA.		
Donald is a higher rate taxpayer. On 6 April 2020 he is to be provided with a petrol driven company car with CO_2 emissions of 57 g/km and a list price of £16,000. Contributing £3,000 towards the cost of the car will save Donald income tax in a year of less than £168.		

TASK 9 (10 marks)

(a) Paul inherited seven acres of land in August 2016 from his grandfather.

The land had cost his grandfather £15,000 but was worth £49,000 (the probate value) when Paul received it.

Paul sold three acres in November 2020 for £75,000 when the remaining four acres were worth £125,000. He paid auctioneer's commission of 8% when he sold the land.

What is the gain on this land? **(3 marks)**

```
┌──────────────────────────────┐
│                              │
└──────────────────────────────┘
```

(b) Artem bought a holiday home in March 2015 for £174,000 plus legal fees of £3,480.

He spent £20,000 on extending the property in April 2017. He has paid insurance premiums totalling £3,750 during the time she has owned the asset.

He sold the property at auction for £355,000 in March 2021 incurring selling costs of £6,500. Artem was disappointed with this price as the property had been valued at £400,000 before the auction.

What is the gain on this asset? **(2 marks)**

```
┌──────────────────────────────┐
│                              │
└──────────────────────────────┘
```

(c) Accountancy fees for calculating capital gains tax are an allowable selling expense when disposing of an asset.

Select whether the above statement is true or false. **(1 mark)**

(d) Rose disposed of the following assets in 2020/21.

For each asset, calculate the gain before the annual exempt amount or the allowable loss:
(4 marks)

(i) Sold a racehorse for £25,000. She had originally purchased the racehorse for £8,900.	£
(ii) Sold an antique table to her neighbour for £5,000. She paid £50 commission on the sale. She originally purchased the table for £11,000. The table got scratched while she owned it (hence the low proceeds).	£
(iii) Sold a holiday cottage in Devon for £110,000. She originally purchased the cottage for £50,000 and extended it two years later which cost £8,000.	£

TASK 10 (10 marks)

Paul disposed of 9,000 shares in Sun Ltd for £5 per share in October 2020.

He acquired the shares as follows:

		Number of shares	Cost
October 2015	Purchase	1,000	£1,250
January 2016	Purchase	3,000	£6,300
December 2017	Bonus issue	1 for 3	
January 2018	Purchase	5,000	£15,200

Clearly showing the balance of shares, and their value, to carry forward calculate the gain or loss made on these shares.

All workings must be shown in your calculations. **(10 marks)**

TASK 11 (7 marks)

(a)   Hamza bought a house for £101,000 on 1 March 1998.

He lived in the house with his wife until 31 March 2002 when they went to work in Newcastle.

He returned to the house on 1 April 2012 and lived in it until 31 July 2019 when he moved in with his elderly parents.

The house was sold for £336,000 on 30 April 2020.

What is the taxable gain assuming Hamza has no other disposals in 2019/20?   (3 marks)

(b)   Magda has disposed of several capital assets in 2020/21 and realised the following gains and losses:

	Disposal to:	£
Chargeable gain	Aunt	23,000
Chargeable gain	Unconnected person	14,800
Allowable loss	Brother	(3,000)
Allowable loss	Friend	(2,600)

Magda had capital gains and losses relating to 2019/20 of £20,000 and £25,600 respectively. The AEA for 2019/20 is £12,000.

Answer the following questions regarding Magda's gains in 2020/21.   (2 marks)

(i)   What are Magda's taxable gains for 2020/21?   £ | |

(ii)   What is the capital loss remaining to carry forward to 2021/22?   £ | |

(c)   Charbel has taxable income of £35,500 for 2020/21. He has made gains of £26,800 on the sale of shares.

Answer the following questions regarding Currie's gains in 2020/21.   (2 marks)

(i)   What is Currie's capital gains tax liability for 2020/21?   £ | |

(ii)   What is the due date of payment? | |

TASK 12 (6 marks)

(a)   **Complete the following sentences using the words on the right.**   **(3 marks)**

Tick the appropriate column for each of the sentences.

	will	will not

1   Pasternak died on 1 June 2020.

On 1 February 2015 Pasternak had given £400,000 to his son.

Pasternak's son ....have to pay inheritance tax in respect of this gift.

	not resident in the UK	not domiciled in the UK	not resident and not domiciled in the UK

2   Quintus owns an investment property in New Zealand.

This property will not be subject to UK inheritance tax when Quintus dies provided Quintus is ....

	was	was not

3   On 1 January 2018 Romanov gave his private residence to his son and set off to travel the world.

Romanov had owned the house for nine years and had lived in it throughout this period of ownership.

On 1 November 2020 Romanov died.

The gift of the house ....an exempt transfer for the purposes of inheritance tax.

(b)   Stanislav died on 15 October 2020.

In the seven years prior to his death Stanislav had made gross chargeable transfers of £160,000.

Stanislav's wife had died on 1 August 2013. Once the inheritance tax payable in respect of her estate had been calculated, there was 44% of her nil rate band remaining.

What is the nil rate band available to set against Stanislav's death estate?   **(1 mark)**

(c)   Are the following statements true or false in connection with inheritance tax?

Tick the appropriate column for each of the sentences.   **(2 marks)**

	True	False
The marriage exemption is available in respect of lifetime gifts only.		
Taper relief is only available in respect of chargeable lifetime transfers made more than three but less than seven years prior to the donor's death.		

TASK 13 (6 marks)

(a)   Tarantella died on 1 December 2020. Her estate was valued at £2,350,000 and did not include any residential property. In her will, Tarantella left £20,000 to a UK charity, £1,600,000 to her husband, and the residue of her estate to her daughter.

In the seven years prior to her death, Tarantella had made gross chargeable transfers of £410,000.

Calculate the inheritance tax payable in respect of Tarantella's estate.

All workings must be shown in your calculations.   **(3 marks)**

(b)   On 1 August 2018, Urban made a gift of £360,000 to his son. Urban died on 1 October 2020. The gift on 1 August 2018 was Urban's only lifetime gift.

Calculate the inheritance tax payable in respect of the gift on 1 August 2018 as a result of Urban's death.

All workings must be shown in your calculations.   **(3 marks)**

Section 4

MOCK ASSESSMENT ANSWERS

TASK 1

Thelma – Professional conduct in relation to taxation

Thelma's argument that the dividend income is not material cannot be sustained. The term materiality relates to the preparation of accounts and not to the reporting of income in a tax return.

It is Thelma's responsibility to submit a tax return that is correct and complete to the best of her knowledge and belief, i.e. including her dividend income.

It is then our firm's responsibility to ensure that the return is accurately based on the information we have received from Thelma. In addition, due to the duty of confidentiality, we must not inform HM Revenue and Customs of Thelma's dividend income without authorisation from her.

One of the fundamental principles with which a member of AAT must comply is integrity, which requires us to be straightforward and honest. We must not be associated with the presentation of facts that we know to be incorrect.

We must act correctly from the outset and keep records of any discussions and our advice. We should first advise Thelma that the dividend income must be included in her tax return.

If Thelma is unwilling to include the dividend income in her tax return, we should advise her of any interest or penalties that may be imposed and the implications for her of not disclosing this information.

If Thelma refuses to disclose this information, we must cease to act for her. We should inform HM Revenue and Customs that we no longer act for her but we should not provide them with any reasons for our actions.

Finally, we should consider our obligations under the anti-money laundering legislation and the necessity to make a suspicious activity report.

TASK 2

(i)	What is the appropriate percentage for Mandeep's Ford car?	30%	W1
(ii)	What is the taxable benefit for the use of the Ford car?	£1,375	W2
(iii)	What is the taxable benefit for the fuel provided by the company?	£3,063	W3
(iv)	What is the appropriate percentage for Mandeep's wife's car?	12%	W4
(v)	What price is used to calculate the car benefit on Mandeep's wife's car?	£12,000	W5
(vi)	What is the taxable benefit for Mandeep's wife's car?	£480	W6

Workings

(W1) Ford appropriate percentage

CO_2 emissions are rounded down to 115 g/km.

Appropriate percentage = (14% + 4% diesel + (115 – 55) × 1/5) = 30%

(W2) Ford taxable benefit

Car has been available for 5 months of the tax year.

	£
£15,000 × 30% × 5/12	1,875
Less: Contribution in respect of private use (£100 × 5 months)	(500)
Car benefit	1,375

Tutorial note

The car has CO_2 emissions in excess of 95 g/km.

The appropriate percentage is therefore calculated in the normal way (i.e. 14% for petrol cars plus 4% for diesel cars, plus 1% for each complete 5 g/km above 45 g/km up to a maximum percentage of 37%).

As the car has not been available all year, the benefit must be time apportioned.

Contributions in respect of the private use of the car are an allowable deduction from the benefit.

(W3) Ford fuel benefit

Fuel benefit = (£24,500 × 30% × 5/12) = £3,063

Tutorial note

The appropriate percentage for the fuel benefit is the same as that calculated for the car benefit. This is applied to a fixed scale figure of £24,500.

As the fuel was not provided all year, the benefit must be time apportioned.

A contribution towards the provision of private fuel is not an allowable deduction from the benefit.

(W4) Mandeep's wife's car appropriate percentage

Appropriate percentage = 12%.

Tutorial note

The car has CO_2 emissions of between 1g/km to 50g/km. To determine the appropriate percentage we must also identify the electric range. For a range between 30 to 39 miles, the percentage is 10%. As this car was registered before 6 April 2020, an additional 2% must be added to this figure.

(W5) Mandeep's wife's car price

Price used to calculate the car benefit = £12,000.

Tutorial note

The second hand price actually paid by the company is not relevant. The car benefit is based on the manufacturer's original list price.

(W6) Mandeep's wife's car – taxable benefit

Car has been available for 4 months of the tax year.

	£
(£12,000 × 12% × 4/12)	480

Tutorial note

This benefit is taxable on Oliver as it is provided by his employer, even though it is used by his wife.

(W7) Mandeep's car price 2021/22

Price used to calculate the car benefit = £15,000.

Tutorial note

Optional accessories added after purchase only increase the value used in the car benefit calculation if the cost of the accessories is ≥ £100.

TASK 3

(a)

(i)	Carol's employer paid £6,700 to cover the costs she incurred when she relocated from Newcastle to Hull in order to start work in her new job.	£Nil	W1
(ii)	Bill received £1,800 as a loan from his employer throughout 2020/21. He pays interest on the loan at the rate of 2%.	£Nil	W2
(iii)	Les borrowed a digital camera from his employer on 6 June 2020 until 5 April 2021 to use on his holidays and for family occasions. The market value of the camera on 6 June 2020 was £1,200.	£200	W3
(iv)	From 6 January 2020, Sarah was provided with a company loan of £22,000 on which she pays interest at 1.75% per annum.	£41	W4
(v)	Majid was provided with accommodation by his employer. The house has an annual value £4,200 and the employer pays a rent of £250 per month. His employer also paid a utility bill for the house of £180 during 2020/21. Majid moved out when he left his employment on 5 December 2020.	£2,980	W5

Workings

(W1) Relocation costs

Taxable benefit = £Nil

Tutorial note

Removal expenses of up to £8,000 are exempt when incurred in relation to a new employment or if an employee's job is relocated.

(W2) Company loan

Taxable benefit = £Nil

Tutorial note

Loans that do not exceed £10,000 at any time in the tax year are an exempt benefit.

(W3) Use of camera

Taxable benefit = (£1,200 × 20% × 10/12) = £200

Tutorial note

The benefit for the use of a company asset such as a camera is 20% of the market value of the asset when first made available to the employee.

As the camera was only made available to Les from 6 June 2020, the benefit is time apportioned.

(W4) Company loan

Taxable benefit = (£22,000 × (2.25% − 1.50%) × 3/12) = £41

Tutorial note

Beneficial loan interest benefit is calculated as follows:

= Outstanding loan × the difference between the official rate of interest (2.25% in 2020/21) and the actual interest rate paid by the employee.

However, as the loan was provided nine months into the tax year 2020/21, the benefit must be time apportioned, as the rates of interest quoted are annual rates of interest.

(W5) Accommodation benefit

	£
Higher of:	
(i) Annual value = £4,200	
Rent paid by employer = (£250 × 12) = £3,000	
Only available for 8 months of the year:	
Basic charge benefit = (£4,200 × 8/12)	2,800
Utility bill paid for by employer – benefit = cost to employer	180
Total accommodation benefit	2,980

(b)   Rose has asked you to advise her which of the following benefits are exempt.

Tick one box on each line.

	Exempt	Not exempt
Private use of a company car that was first registered on 6 April 2020 with CO_2 emissions of 52 g/km		✓
A place in the company's workplace based nursery for two children	✓	
A second mobile telephone for the spouse of each employee		✓
Provision of bicycle helmets for staff earning below £20,000 p.a.		✓
Staff Christmas party costing £75 per employee	✓	
Relocation expenses of £7,500	✓	

Tutorial note

A car with CO_2 emissions between 51 g/km and 55 g/km will lead to a taxable benefit. The appropriate % will be 13% for a petrol car and 17% for a diesel car that does not meet the RDE2 standards.

A place in the workplace nursery is an exempt benefit, regardless of the number of children or cost of provision. The limits that apply depending on the rate of tax the employee pays relate to childcare vouchers used with approved carers other than in the workplace nursery.

Only one mobile phone per employee is treated as an exempt benefit.

The provision of cycle helmets is an exempt benefit provided they are available to all staff generally. It will not be exempt if it is conditional on the amount earned.

Staff entertaining of up to £150 per head per tax year is an exempt benefit.

Relocation expenses of up to £8,000 are an exempt benefit.

TASK 4

(a)   Which of the following statements are true and which false?

Tick the correct box for each statement.

	True	False
Income tax is always charged at 0% on the first £2,000 of a taxpayer's dividend income.	✓	
An individual who receives annual pension income of £19,000, will pay income tax of £1,200 on savings income of £6,000 in 2020/21.		✓
A higher rate taxpayer receives interest from an ISA of £600. The £600 received is exempt from income tax.	✓	

Tutorial note

The second statement is false because it fails to take account of the savings income allowance of £1,000 that will be available as the taxpayer is a basic rate taxpayer (taxable income of £19,000 + £6,000 - £12,500 = £12,500). The personal allowance is utilised by the pension income, then the first £1,000 of savings income is covered by the savings income allowance. The remaining £5,000 of savings income is taxed at 20%, i.e. tax of £1,000.

(b)   Total tax payable in respect of investment income

Polly

The answer is £2,480.

Polly's salary after the personal allowance is £82,200 (£88,000 + £6,700 - £12,500). This means she is a higher rate taxpayer.   Her savings allowance is £500, thus the first £500 of her interest income is taxed at 0%. The remainder is taxed at 40% (her taxable salary after the personal allowance is £75,500 so this will have used the basic rate band in full. The total tax payable is therefore £2,480 ((£6,700 – £500) × 40%).

Priscilla

The answer is £1,562.

Priscilla is an additional rate taxpayer due to the level of her other income. She is not entitled to a personal allowance as her adjusted net income is greater than £125,000. The first £2,000 of her dividend income is taxed at 0% due to the dividend allowance. The remainder is taxed at 38.1%. The total tax payable is therefore £1,562 ((£6,100 – £2,000) × 38.1%).

Priti

The answer is £625.

Priti is not entitled to a personal allowance as her adjusted net income is greater than £125,000. She is an additional rate taxpayer as her taxable income exceeds £150,000 (£149,000 + £1,500); thus she has no savings allowance. The savings income that falls into the higher rate band, which is £1,000 (£150,000 - £149,000), is taxed at 40% and the remaining £500 is taxed at 45%. The total tax payable is therefore £625 ((£1,000 × 40%) + £500 × 45%).

TASK 5

	Four bedroom house £	One bedroom flat £	Two bedroom house £
Income	9,360	3,795	5,490
Expenses:			
Dining furniture	2,040		
Commission	655		
Cleaning		660	
Roof repairs			280
Profit or Loss	6,665	3,135	5,210

Workings

	Four bedroom house	One bedroom Flat	Two bedroom house
	£	£	£
Income:			
(£780 × 12 months)	9,360		
(£415 × 6 months)		2,490	
(£435 × 3 months)		1,305	
		3,795	
(£610 × 9 months)			5,490
Expenses:			
Dining furniture	(2,040)		
£2,040 (£2,200 – £160)			
Agents commission (7% × £9,360)	(655)		
Cleaning (£60 × 11)		(660)	
Roof repairs			(280)
Rental profit	6,665	3,135	5,210

Tutorial note

As the gross rents do not exceed £150,000 rental income is assessed on a cash basis; therefore, only the rent received should be brought into the computation. The accruals basis will be used if an election is made to do so, or if gross rents are higher than this figure for the year.

The expenses actually paid in the tax year are deductible, therefore one month of cleaning will not be deducted until 2021/22 and the roof repairs are deducted in 2020/21, although they were not carried out until 2021/22.

The allowable deduction in respect of the replacement of the dining furniture is restricted to £2,040 (£2,200 – £160), being the cost of furniture of a similar standard less the proceeds received in respect of the sale of the old furniture.

The property allowance is not relevant for Steven as his rent and expenses both exceed £1,000.

TASK 6

Rita – Income tax computation – 2020/21

	Non-savings	Dividends	Total
	£	£	£
Salary	33,030		
Bonus (received 21 April 2020)	4,435		
Employment income	37,465		37,465
Dividends		13,025	13,025
ISA interest – exempt			Nil
Net income	37,465	13,025	50,490
Less: PA	(12,500)		(12,500)
Taxable income	24,965	13,025	37,990

Income tax:

		Total
Non-savings income – basic rate	24,965 × 20%	4,993
Dividend income – dividend allowance	2,000 × 0%	0
Dividend income – basic rate	10,535 × 7.5%	790
	37,500	
Dividend income	490 × 32.5%	159
	37,990	
Income tax liability		5,942
Less : PAYE		(4,993)
Income tax payable		949

Key answer tips

It is important when using this type of layout to analyse the taxable income into 'non-savings income', 'savings' and 'dividends' as different rates of tax apply to the different sources of income.

Note that:

- the above layout should be possible if the CBA gives five columns to complete the calculation

- the total lines cannot be inserted in the real CBA

- you may find it useful to do the computation on paper first before inputting on screen.

You may only be provided with three columns in the CBA. If this is the case, you may find it useful to write your answer up on paper first using all five columns, then type the total column only into the profoma.

TASK 7

(a)   The answer is £5,320.00

            Working   £

	£
(£50,000 – £9,500) × 12%	4,860.00
(£73,000 – £50,000) × 2%	460.00
	5,320.00

(b)   The answer is £8,861.26

            Working

(£73,000 – £8,788) × 13.8%	£8,861.26

(c)   The answer is £1,062.60.

Working	£
Benefit in respect of company car	7,700
Workplace childcare	0
	7,700
£7,700 × 13.8%	1,062.60

Tutorial note

No deduction is available for expenses incurred wholly, exclusively and necessarily in the performance of duties when calculating earnings for the purposes of national insurance contributions.

The workplace childcare is an exempt benefit, such that it is not subject to class 1A contributions.

TASK 8

(a)   (i)   £360

                Both Niamh and Roberto can invest £20,000 into an ISA in 2020/21. The interest earned will then be exempt from income tax, and will therefore save Niamh tax on that interest at 40% and Roberto tax on the interest at 20%. The tax saving will be £480 (£20,000 × 3% × 40%) + (£20,000 × 3% × 20%).

       (ii)   £400

                Roberto is a basic rate taxpayer, and therefore has an unused savings allowance of £1,000. By transferring enough of her investment to Roberto to utilise this allowance, Niamh will save tax of £400 (£1,000 × 40%).

(iii)   £1,200

Roberto has taxable income of £30,500. He therefore has an unused basic rate band of £7,000 (£37,500 - £30,500). £1,000 of this basic rate band will be utilised by the £1,000 covered by his savings allowance as mentioned above. He therefore has a further £6,000 of basic rate band available. Any savings income falling in this band will be taxed at 20% for Roberto, rather than 40% for Niamh. By transferring a further amount of her investment to Roberto to utilise this band, Niamh will save tax of £1,200 (£6,000 × (40% − 20%).

Tutorial note

Niamh's own savings allowance of £500 will be used by her existing savings income.

(b)

	True	False
There is no upper limit on the amount of tax-free chargeable gains which can be made by a taxpayer in a tax year in respect of shares held in an ISA.	✓	
Donald is a higher rate taxpayer. He is about to be provided with a petrol driven company car with CO_2 emissions of 57 g/km and a list price of £16,000. Contributing £3,000 towards the cost of the car will save Donald income tax in a year of less than £168.	✓	

Tutorial note

In the second statement, Donald's tax saving would be £168 (£3,000 × 14% × 40%).

TASK 9

(a)   The answer is £50,625.

	£
Proceeds	75,000
Less: Auction fees (£75,000 × 8%)	(6,000)
	69,000
Less: Cost £49,000 × (£75,000/(£75,000 + £125,000))	(18,375)
Chargeable gain	50,625

Tutorial note

If a taxpayer inherits an asset, its cost when calculating the chargeable gain on its disposal is its value at death; also referred to as the probate value.

Note that this rule is similar to receiving a gift where the cost is the market value at the date of receipt.

With a part disposal of the land, the cost must be apportioned using the A/A+B formula NOT on the proportion of acreage sold.

Note that A is the gross sale proceeds, before deducting the auction fees.

(b)   The answer is £151,020.

		£
Proceeds		355,000
Less: Selling costs		(6,500)
		348,500
Less: Cost (£174,000 + £3,480)		(177,480)
Extension		(20,000)
Chargeable gain		151,020

Tutorial note

If a taxpayer sells an asset in an arm's length sale, as is the case with an auction, it does not matter that the market value may be different to the actual proceeds. The actual proceeds must be used in the computation.

Insurance premiums are not an allowable cost for capital gains purposes.

(c)   This statement is false.

(d)   (i)   Gain on racehorse

(ii)   Allowable loss on antique table (W1)

(iii)   Gain on holiday cottage (W2)

£Nil
£5,050
£52,000

Tutorial note

A racehorse is a wasting chattel and is exempt from capital gains tax.

Workings

(W1) Antique table

	£
Deemed proceeds	6,000
Less: Selling costs	(50)
	5,950
Less: Cost	(11,000)
Allowable loss	(5,050)

Tutorial note

An antique table is a non-wasting chattel and as it cost > £6,000 and proceeds are < £6,000, special rules apply.

The gross proceeds are deemed to be £6,000 in the allowable loss calculation.

(W2) Holiday cottage

	£
Proceeds	110,000
Less: Cost	(50,000)
Extension	(8,000)
Chargeable gain	52,000

TASK 10

Chargeable gain calculation

	£
Proceeds (9,000 × £5)	45,000
Less: Cost (W)	(19,815)
Chargeable gain	25,185

Working: Share pool

		Number	Cost £
Oct 2015	Purchase	1,000	1,250
Jan 2016	Purchase	3,000	6,300
		4,000	7,550
Dec 2017	Bonus issue (1 for 3)	1,333	Nil
Jan 2018	Purchase	5,000	15,200
		10,333	22,750
Oct 2020	Sale (£22,750 × 9,000/10,333)	(9,000)	(19,815)
Balance c/f		1,333	2,935

TASK 11

(a)   The answer is £19,805.

	£
Sale proceeds	336,000
Less: Cost	(101,000)
	235,000
Less: PRR (£235,000 × 230/266) (W)	(203,195)
Chargeable gain	31,805
Less: AEA	(12,300)
Taxable gain	19,505

Working: PPR relief

		Total months	Exempt months	Chargeable months
1 Mar 1998 — 31 Mar 2002	Owner occupied	49	49	
1 Apr 2002 — 31 Mar 2012	Working in Newcastle	120	84 (Note 1)	36
1 Apr 2012 — 31 Jul 2019	Owner occupied	88	88	
1 Jul 2019 — 30 April 2020	Empty	9	9 (Note 2)	
		266	230	36

Tutorial note

1   Of the 120 months working in Newcastle, a maximum of 48 months are deemed occupation as 'working elsewhere in the UK'.

A further 36 months are then allowed as deemed occupation for any reason – as this period is both preceded and followed by periods of actual occupation by Harold.

Total period of deemed occupation is therefore 84 months (48 + 36).

2   The last nine months of ownership is always allowed.

If asked for taxable gain remember to deduct the annual exempt amount!

(b)   (i)   **Taxable gain**

		£
Chargeable gains (£23,000 + £14,800)		37,800
Less: Current year allowable losses (Note)		(2,600)
		35,200
Less: Annual exempt amount		(12,300)
		22,900
Less: Capital losses brought forward		(5,600)
Taxable gain		17,300

(ii)   **Capital loss left to carry forward**

Loss on disposal to brother (Note)		3,000

Tutorial note

The loss arising on the disposal to the brother is a connected person loss.

It cannot be set against other gains. It can only be carried forward and set against gains arising from disposals to the same brother in the future.

The 2019/20 capital losses are automatically set off as far as possible against the 2019/20 gains. This means £20,000 of the losses were utilised in 2019/20 and the AEA is wasted. The remaining capital losses of £5,600 are carried forward and offset against future net gains after the deduction of the AEA.

(c) (i) **Capital gains tax liability**

	£
Capital gains	26,800
Less: Annual exempt amount	(12,300)
Taxable gains	14,500

£		
2,000 (W)	× 10%	200
12,500	× 20%	2,500
14,500		2,700

Working

	£
Basic rate band	37,500
Less: Taxable income	(35,500)
Basic rate band unused	2,000

Tutorial note

Chargeable gains are taxed at 10% if they fall below the basic rate threshold and 20% if they fall above the threshold.

(ii) The due date of payment is 31 January 2022.

TASK 12

(a) Complete the following sentences using the words on the right.

	will	will not
1 Pasternak died on 1 June 2020. On 1 February 2015 Pasternak had given £400,000 to his son. Pasternak's son ....have to pay inheritance tax in respect of this gift.	✓	

	not resident in the UK	not domiciled in the UK	not resident and not domiciled in the UK
2 Quintus owns an investment property in New Zealand. This property will not be subject to UK inheritance tax when Quintus dies provided Quintus is		✓	

	was	was not
3 On 1 January 2018 Romanov gave his private residence to his son and set off to travel the world. Romanov had owned the house for nine years and had lived in it throughout this period of ownership. On 1 November 2020 Romanov died. The gift of the house ....an exempt transfer for the purposes of inheritance tax.		✓

Tutorial note

1   *Pasternak has died within seven years of making a potentially exempt transfer to his son, such that inheritance tax will be payable. The inheritance tax due in respect of a potentially exempt transfer is payable by the donee.*

2   *An individual who is not domiciled in the UK is subject to UK inheritance tax on UK assets only. The concept of residence is not relevant for inheritance tax purposes.*

3   *A private residence is an exempt asset for the purposes of capital gains tax but not for the purposes of inheritance tax.*

(b)   The answer is £308,000.

	£
Nil rate band at the date of death	325,000
Nil rate band transferred from wife (£325,000 × 44%)	143,000
Stanislav's gross chargeable transfers in the seven years prior to death	(160,000)
Nil rate band available to Stanislav	308,000

(c)   Are the following statements true or false in connection with inheritance tax?

	True	False
The marriage exemption is available in respect of lifetime gifts only.	✓	
Taper relief is only available in respect of chargeable lifetime transfers made more than three but less than seven years prior to the donor's death.		✓

Tutorial note

*Taper relief is available in respect of **all** lifetime gifts made more than three but less than seven years prior to the donor's death, i.e. including potentially exempt transfers.*

TASK 13

(a)   Tarantella

	£
Value of estate	2,350,000
Less: Exempt legacy to spouse	(1,600,000)
Exempt legacy to charity	(20,000)
Chargeable amount	730,000
Nil rate band (£325,000 – £410,000)	Nil
Taxable amount	730,000
Inheritance tax (£730,000 × 40%)	292,000

(b)   Urban

	£
Gift	360,000
Less: Annual exemption for 2018/19	(3,000)
Annual exemption for 2017/18	(3,000)
Chargeable amount	354,000
Nil rate band	(325,000)
Taxable amount	29,000
Inheritance tax (£29,000 × 40%)	11,600

Tutorial note

Taper relief is not available because Urban died within three years of making the gift.